BETHEL

MAINE

BETHEL
MAINE
A BRIEF HISTORY

Stanley Russell Howe

The History Press

Published by The History Press
Charleston, SC 29403
www.historypress.net

Front cover, bottom: *Saddleback* [Baldpate] *From Bethel Hill*, 1875; oil painting by J. Spaulding Record, courtesy Bethel Historical Society.

All images courtesy of the Bethel Historical Society unless otherwise noted.

First published 2009

Manufactured in the United States

ISBN 978.1.59629.710.4

Library of Congress CIP data applied for.

Notice: The information in this book is true and complete to the best of our knowledge. It is offered without guarantee on the part of the author or The History Press. The author and The History Press disclaim all liability in connection with the use of this book.

CONTENTS

ACKNOWLEDGEMENTS

This book is the product of years of research. I am grateful to all those who came before me for their contributions to Bethel's history. A great effort has been made on my part to ensure the accuracy of the information contained here. I am also grateful to all those who read the text and made useful comments. These individuals included Arlan and Eleanor Jodrey, Edna York, Randall Bennett, Danna Nickerson, Jay Boschetti, Rosalind Chapman and Kent Taylor. I am also indebted to those who provided photographs (especially the Bethel Historical Society) and information during the preparation of this book. Much gratitude is also due Randall Bennett for his help in scanning photographs and illustrations. In addition, his advice throughout the writing and production process has also been most valuable. Naturally, any errors or deficiencies that remain must rest on my shoulders, for which I beg forgiveness. Historical writing is an ongoing process, and those who follow us have every incentive to build upon the foundation that our generation has been privileged to inherit and enlarge upon.

Chapter One

EARLY BETHEL

Bethel's historic roots extend back to the struggle between France and Britain in the 1680s for control of the North American continent. It was also a rivalry between Catholics and Protestants. The French in the New World did not hesitate to attack outlying settlements, particularly those in what is today New Hampshire and Maine. Responding to these threats, the General Court of Massachusetts was determined to re-conquer Nova Scotia and to bring Quebec into submission. It sent the seasoned military leader Sir William Phipps to lead a 1690 expedition of ships and men that succeeded easily in Nova Scotia, but failed dismally in Quebec. This and other defense campaigns bankrupted the commonwealth, and the only course open to colonial officials appeared to be making land grants in its District of Maine. Nothing happened for a variety of reasons, however, for more than seventy years until a solicitor, Josiah Richardson, succeeded in 1768 in obtaining a land grant. It came to be called Sudbury Canada, since its name designated the town in Massachusetts (Sudbury) where the veterans had originated and Canada identified the campaign in which they had participated. It was located in what was then York County on both sides of the Androscoggin River and measured about "six and three-quarters miles square."

None of the original grantees lived long enough to settle in Sudbury Canada. Most had died during the intervening years between 1690 and 1768. Some sold their holdings, while others let their claims be resolved for taxes. Originally, the grant represented over fifty thousand acres. Later, part of the original grant north of the Androscoggin River was ceded to become part of the town of Hanover when it separated from Bethel in 1843.

No one knows who was the first Euro-American to come to what is today Bethel to stay for any length of time. A number of people were here for

Bethel.

Engraving of one of Bethel's most spectacular mountain vistas from the 1853 *Guidebook of the Atlantic and St. Lawrence Railroad. Courtesy of Randall H. Bennett.*

sugaring operations and other seasonal pursuits, but it is nearly impossible to determine the identity of many of the early settlers until what has been termed "New England's Last Indian Raid" occurred in 1781.

On August 3, 1781, during the American War for Independence, six Indians—led by Tomhegan, who was well known to the settlers—came down from Quebec to Umbagog Lake and through the Bear River Valley, plundering settlers' houses along the way. According to Nathaniel Segar's account, published in 1825, the Indians were painted and heavily armed. There were only ten families here at that time, plus four single men. These included Captain Eleazer Twitchell (1744–1818), a miller; Lieutenant Jonathan Clark (1746–1821); Benjamin Clark, unmarried (1759–1802); John Grover; Peter Austin; Abraham Russell (1748–1839); James Swan (1721–1800); Benjamin Russell (1739–1802); Amos Hastings, married, but his family remained in Fryeburg (1757–1829); David Marshall; Colonel John York; Jesse Dustin; Amos Powers (1732–1823); and Nathaniel Segar, unmarried (1755–1847). Jonathan Clark, Nathaniel Segar and Eleazer Twitchell were working near the woods at Clark's house when they were suddenly captured. The Indians then began to plunder Clark's house, where they discovered rum and money. Another Indian who was trailing behind the main war party captured Benjamin Clark. Shortly after this, Eleazer Twitchell, seeing his chance, escaped and hid in the woods near what is today Kimball Park. The prisoners were then loaded with plunder and forced to leave with their arms bound to their sides.

Arriving in what is today Shelburne, New Hampshire, two new prisoners were added to the group. The Sudbury Canada men were then given an opportunity to select one of their fellow settlers to be released. Lieutenant Clark, an older man with a family, was so designated and allowed to return home. The Indians admonished him to stay on the trail and not to warn anyone or else the prisoners would be killed. Clark was savvy enough to know that he probably would be killed and scalped if he stayed on the trail, so he crossed the river without being discovered and after a few days arrived safely back in Sudbury Canada. The British were then paying the Indians eight dollars per prisoner or scalp to disrupt outlying American settlements. They already had three, and undoubtedly Clark's would have been next since a couple of Indians were bringing up the rear. It took two weeks for the Indians and their prisoners to arrive in Quebec, where they were later incarcerated for eighteen months.

Meanwhile, back in Sudbury Canada, panic took hold of those remaining inhabitants. A plea for a rescue expedition was sent to Fryeburg for assistance. A company of thirty men, with the friendly Indian Sabbatis as guide, marched single file forty miles to Captain Twitchell's house in Sudbury Canada. The next morning, the men followed in pursuit of the Indians and their prisoners. Fortunately, they never caught up with them, as some of the settlers would have been killed; the men then returned to Sudbury Canada.

So alarmed by this attack were the settlers of Sudbury Canada that two modest fortifications were erected for protection against further raids. One was built near Captain Twitchell's house on Mill Brook in what became known as the West Parish and another near Colonel John York's farm in the East Parish. During the day, men carried guns as they went about their work; one shot was announced as the signal for flight to the forts, but no alarm ever came. The Fryeburg soldiers went home and later, in October of that year, General Cornwallis surrendered to General George Washington, ending the war. All expense borne by the settlers in building the forts and the roads to connect them, as well as paying Captain Farrington's Fryeburg troops, was never reimbursed by the General Court of Massachusetts as promised.

Benjamin Clark and Nathaniel Segar were held in a Quebec jail on an island in the St. Lawrence River until November 10, 1782, when they were

Sugaring scene. *Author's collection.*

Nathaniel Segar gravestone, Hanover Cemetery, Hanover, Maine.

placed onboard a vessel bound for Boston. Their families had all but given up hope of seeing them again when they appeared in their former homes in Newton, Massachusetts. After several weeks of recuperation, they both headed back to their claims in Sudbury Canada. Segar promptly married Mary Russell, daughter of Benjamin, and they became parents of thirteen children in what is today Hanover. Benjamin Clark soon married Betsy Mason (1754–1846) from the Mayville section of the plantation. She and her husband settled in the Skillingston neighborhood and became parents of eight children.

Following the Revolution, Sudbury Canada grew rapidly with families seeking good agricultural land and settling on the rich intervales along the Androscoggin River. A major event four years later, in 1785, was the "Great Flood," which washed away and destroyed almost all of the houses and farms of Sudbury Canada. The intervale lands originally cleared by the Indians, who by the time the white settlers arrived had largely disappeared from the area, seemed to ease the rigors of settlement. However, the inhabitants apparently possessed little idea that the Androscoggin could at times be

East Bethel intervales looking north into present-day Hanover.

very threatening to life and property. A move to higher ground above the intervales brought relief from this danger and is where most people continue to live.

By the time of the census of 1790, Sudbury Canada claimed sixty families, totaling 326 residents. By 1796, the settlement reached enough population to seek town status. Bethel was incorporated on June 10, 1796, as the 107th town in the District of Maine. At the suggestion of Reverend Eliphaz Chapman (1747–1814), Sudbury Canada became "Bethel" from the book of Genesis, meaning "House of God." Reverend Chapman would soon be the first representative from Bethel to the Massachusetts General Court. The first town meeting was held in Amos Hastings's barn or house (accounts vary) in Middle Intervale in the East Parish on August 15, 1796.

At incorporation, the town center was at Middle Intervale. It was very much an agrarian community, with a string of businesses such as cheese and potash factories and stores along what is today Intervale Road, but it had no real waterpower, which in most cases was essential to settlement. About 1845, the town built a town house, just over the parish line in the East

Middle Intervale Meetinghouse, built in 1816.

Parish, which stood until the 1870s, when it was dismantled and reused in the construction of the present Bonnema Potters' barn. At Bethel Hill, in the West Parish, there was water power, but of a limited nature.

As was the case with most New England towns, the Congregational church dominated religious life, but by the late 1790s, Bethel began to have Baptists and Methodists among its populace. The Congregational church established in 1796 was located in the West Parish, first near the Androscoggin River, but after 1847 on Bethel Hill's Church Street. The first settled Congregational minister was Reverend Daniel Gould, a soldier of the Revolution and a Harvard College graduate, who served until 1809. There also was a second Congregational church built after 1849 across the Androscoggin in the Mayville section of Bethel, with Reverend David Garland as the only minister for twenty-five years, or the entire life of that congregation before the merger with the one on Church Street.

The Baptists and the Methodists shared the Middle Intervale Meetinghouse, built in 1816, in the East Parish, until 1858, when the Baptists

First Congregational Meetinghouse, built in 1807, was modeled after Portland's Cumberland County Courthouse of 1785 (shown here).

Dr. Moses Mason House as it appeared about 1900. *Author's collection.*

bought out the Methodists, who then moved to Bethel Hill. Moreover, in the early 1830s, the Baptists also built a church at East Bethel, not far from Bean's corner, also known as the "Lower Meetinghouse," since it was downriver from all other Bethel churches. It later became a Union (or nondenominational) church. At the Hill in the West Parish, the Methodists

erected a steepled church on Main Street in 1859, which was destroyed years later by a strong wind. It was rebuilt and rededicated in 1892. The Methodists had earlier constructed their first church in what is today Hanover near the present Hanover Cemetery. It was later converted into a furniture factory. The Methodists also were involved in the construction in North Bethel of the Locke Meetinghouse in the early nineteenth century. There was also a Free Will Baptist Church built at West Bethel in 1844, which had, according to historian Dr. Nathaniel Tuckerman True (1812–1887), fifty-four members in 1874.

The Universalists Society was organized in 1847, and in 1853 its members built a house of worship on Church Street in the West Parish, with Reverend Zenas Thompson serving as its first minister. The West Bethel Union Church dates from 1897 and was built for the Ladies Aid Society by local entrepreneur A.S. Bean. Later churches included the Christian Science, built in 1924 on Chapman Street and closed in 1949. It became the Bethel Masonic Lodge in 1952. Also in this category are the Alliance Church established on Walker's Mills Road in 1979 and the Pleasant Valley Bible Church built in 1980 on the Flat Road.

Schools began to assume importance, and by 1798 there were a dozen district schools. At the time of the Civil War, more than thirty had been built.

Dr. Timothy Carter was the first settled physician in Bethel and practiced from his Middle Intervale brick-end home for more than forty-five years.

Alpheus S. Bean's crew haying, West Bethel, circa 1900. *Courtesy of Danna Brown Nickerson.*

Other physicians who served the town in these early years were Dr. Moses Mason, Dr. John Grover, Dr. Robert G. Wiley and Dr. Almon Twitchell.

William Frye was the first lawyer to settle in town, arriving in 1823 from Fryeburg, and he served faithfully until his death in 1854. His son Richard followed in his footsteps as a lawyer as well.

Farming and logging (particularly in the winter months) were the chief occupations of the inhabitants of the town for much of the nineteenth century. The rich intervale farmland bordering the Androscoggin River was one of the "magnets" that drew settlers to the town. It was these lands that attracted the attention of those who made tours of Maine and recorded their impressions, such as Reverend Paul Coffin of Buxton, who in the late 1790s visited Bethel and praised farmers such as Asa Kimball when noting the abundance of maple sugar in the town. It is also interesting to observe that according to Dr. True, the intervales along the present North Road may have been the site of an Indian village. Eventually, those who came later were forced to clear land on hillsides, where the soil was less fertile and the certainty of success limited. When agriculture began to decline after the Civil War, it was these marginal farms that were among the first to be abandoned and allowed to return to the forests from which they came a generation or two earlier.

Mills and manufacturing have been an integral part of Bethel since its earliest days. Reminders of that distant past come to mind with place

Logging camp scene, circa 1900.

names still used in present-day Bethel, including Walker's Mills, Steam Mill, Skillingston, Mill Hill and Mill Brook. Wood products and dowel mills that were so significant for much of the late nineteenth century and throughout a good deal of the twentieth century are direct descendants of those from this earlier era. In fact, a mill structure was the first framed building erected in the town in the 1770s. In 1774, Eleazer Twitchell, son of Captain Joseph Twitchell, arrived in Sudbury Canada to build the first sawmill and subsequently a gristmill at the bottom of Mill Hill on the brook that flows north into the Androscoggin River. By 1779, a frame house stood near a gristmill on an island created by a split in Mill Brook. This was presumably erected to house millworkers and later the family of Eleazer Twitchell, who embodied the image of the proverbial "jolly miller" with his mills serving as the heart of this tiny settlement. Other mills in town were at South Bethel on Alder River, as well as in the neighborhood that became known as "Skillingston," at Bethel Hill near the depot and at West Bethel. These were developed by such figures as James Walker, C.C. Walker, L.W. Russell, Hosea Ripley, John Harris, Joseph Twitchell, Moses Cross, Jesse Cross, Eber Clough, Eben Kilborn, A.S. Bean, Robbins Brown and his two sons, David and Robbins Jr., and others. The mills in Bethel were involved with carding wool, fulling homespun, sawing lumber, producing starch and shingles, tanning leather and manufacturing dowels, furniture and boxes.

For all of the nineteenth century and well into the twentieth, the town was governed by a three-member Board of Selectmen, Assessors and Overseers of the Poor, who were elected at the annual town meeting. Leadership for this board was placed in the first selectman. Issues faced during this period included roads, schools and the care of the poor. On the latter subject, Bethel held poor auctions (otherwise known as the vendue system) from 1817 until outlawed by the Maine legislature thirty years later, at which the poor were lined up and auctioned off at town meetings to the lowest bidder. The able-bodied poor could be obtained for work on the "buyer's" farm at a much lower price than the elderly and infirm, who often needed extensive care. There were also other difficulties in dealing with the poor. It was usually common practice to include the insane or mentally unbalanced in with the poor. In addition, town officials were vigilant in making certain that any poor arriving in Bethel and requiring support were not from another municipality. If the town of their origin could be determined, Bethel town officials, like their contemporaries in Maine and throughout New England, made every attempt to return them to the place in which they had originated. For example, in 1830, Selectman Israel Kimball (1795–1865), in his role

Mill at South Bethel ("Walker's Mills"), circa 1890.

as overseer of the poor, traveled east over one hundred miles to Bingham, Maine, to return a "pauper" to his home there. Following the abolition of the vendue system, the town meeting directed the appointment of a committee to investigate the possible purchase of a town farm. One was eventually acquired at East Bethel on Kimball Hill but was later sold and another was secured in 1880. The latter farm was formerly owned by Peter Smith and located in North Bethel. It continued to function as a home for the poor for nearly a century, until it was closed and soon after cleared from the site.

One of the most prominent figures in the town at this time was Dr. Moses Mason (1789–1866), who with his wife, the former Agnes Straw (1792–1869), lived in their home overlooking the West Parish Common for over fifty years. Mason gave every indication of resembling a patriarch of the town with, as a contemporary wrote of him, "his long white hair, blue swallowtail coat with brass buttons, buff vest, ruffled shirt and beaver hat." In personal influence, he carried weight not only in Bethel but throughout western Maine and the state as well. He seems also to have been a popular figure during his two terms in Washington, D.C., as U.S. congressman from

Maine. As a young man, his crucial decision to become a medical doctor, departing from the family tradition of farming, allowed him opportunities that might not have come his way had he spent his life in agricultural pursuits. In 1811, he decided to journey to Newfield, Maine, to apprentice under his physician brother-in-law, Dr. James Ayer, to become a medical doctor, teaching school there to support himself. Upon returning to Bethel in April 1813, with his certificate from the Massachusetts Medical Society (Maine was part of Massachusetts until 1820) in hand, he possessed the foresight to construct his house overlooking a spot that would become the center of the young town. His medical practice brought him some prestige, but assuming the station as the town's first postmaster certainly solidified his image in the community as a leading citizen. He was genuinely enthused about the mail service. He recalled toward the end of his life that it had not been the arrival of the railroad in Bethel in 1851 that was the highlight of his life. Instead, when he heard the postal rider's horn for the first time in 1815, it signaled to him that Bethel was indeed connected to the outside world.

In his timing, Dr. Mason was fortunate, since he fit in well with what was going on in the Maine of his era. He was a Baptist at a time when Baptists and Methodists were challenging the established order of Congregationalism. Moreover, as an Anti-Federalist in his political beliefs and later a Jacksonian Democrat, he espoused positions that were widely embraced by the majority of his fellow citizens in the hinterland of Maine following the War of 1812.

Mason's personal qualities also helped him immensely in acquiring his patriarchal bearing. He was genial, generous with his time and always ready to offer sound advice. As a justice of the peace, he was involved in a variety of quasi-legal cases and married over forty couples in his house, endearing himself to numerous brides by collecting the fee from the bridegroom and promptly turning it over to the bride. His political offices—selectman, county commissioner, United States representative from Maine, member of the Governor's Council, trustee of the Insane Hospital, etc.—enhanced his prestige within the town and beyond.

As a builder of mills on Pleasant River beginning in 1827, Dr. Mason's influence among his neighbors grew. Following his return from Congress, he focused his attention largely on mills, giving up medicine and turning to land speculation and business. Eventually, he would operate two gristmills, one carding mill and a shingle mill and own thousands of acres of land. Many of his entrepreneurial operations were located just west of Bethel in a new Maine town that would be named for him in 1843.

Dr. Mason possessed vision and business acumen, but his judgment was not always infallible. His proposal to build a canal from the Androscoggin to Long Lake at Harrison to join the Cumberland and Oxford Canal did not take into account the emerging enthusiasm for rail transportation. This plan would probably have benefited his interests, since the proposed canal appeared likely to pass through his land. The arrival of the Atlantic and St. Lawrence Railroad in 1851 at Bethel effectively killed any chance that the canal would become economically feasible. The doctor's final project, during which he contracted pneumonia and died, involved the landscaping of Woodland Cemetery, which was possibly inspired by New England's great garden cemeteries, among them Mount Auburn in Cambridge, Massachusetts, and Mount Hope in Bangor. Terracing and building contours, planting a variety of shrubs and installing granite curbing were all part of this "labor of love," once again reflecting the doctor's kindly and generous nature in advancing this ambitious project to benefit the community.

Beginning in the 1850s, Dr. Mason opened the grove in back of his Federal-style house every year on the Fourth of July for a community picnic, where patriotic speeches and lively brass band music were featured as long as he lived. In 1993, this tradition was resumed in a more modest way by the Bethel Historical Society, which acquired his house and lot for a headquarters in 1974.

Undoubtedly for later observers, the most famous visitor to pass over the threshold of the Masons' Federal-era home was the famed Indian healer Molly Ockett, who, according to Dr. True's well-known account, asked for and was served only half a glass of rum rather than her usual quantity. Noting this slight had been made with the explanation that it was all that was available, she quickly responded, "J-e-s-t enough!"

Dr. Mason's wife was born in Brentwood, New Hampshire, in 1793. The family later settled in Newfield, Maine, where she met the future doctor in 1811 when he arrived in that town to apprentice under Dr. Ayer. She journeyed to Bethel in January 1814 after her June 1813 marriage to Dr. Mason and lived in the 1813 house for more than half a century. A popular couple, they met many notables during her husband's tenure in Washington when he served in the House of Representatives in the 1830s. Both the doctor and his wife kept autograph books in which they collected a large number of famous names, including several presidents' signatures. In her book is also found an original poem written in January 1835 by former president (and at that time U.S. representative) John Quincy Adams of Massachusetts:

Woodland Cemetery, one of Bethel's most historic places, contains the graves of many nineteenth-century notables.

To Mrs. Mason
What though a stranger holds the pen
To greet thee with the opening year?
Believe him—of the sons of men
None brings a tribute more sincere.

None breathes to heaven a warmer prayer
That all Earth's comforts may be thine
Till passing from this world of care
They brighten into bliss divine.

Whenever this page shall meet thine eye
Let us no longer strangers be;

Repairing the road over a stone culvert, Bethel, circa 1900. *Author's collection.*

Be thine the blessing from on high
And in thy heart remember me.

In addition to her experience in Washington, she also became involved in the 1840s with the movement to eradicate "demon rum" from American society. This crusade achieved national prominence under the leadership of Portlander Neal Dow's leadership with passage of the "Maine Law" by the legislature in 1851. A number of temperance meetings were held at the Mason home in Bethel during their residency.

In the years before Maine statehood in 1820, the roads leading to and within the town began to improve. A highway built in 1797, which connected Paris and Rumford, passed through Bethel's southeast corner. In 1812–13, a road was constructed over Paradise Hill to Norway, giving Bethel Hill access to markets to the south. As settlements grew on both sides of the Androscoggin, difficult fording opportunities were replaced with ferries, which required only the river's current to propel them from one side to the other. The earliest such ferry seems to have been Duston's at East Bethel, which began operations in the 1780s. At one time or another, there were several ferries operating in Bethel: Barker's, Kendall's, Hanover and West Bethel. Ferries were seasonal, so building bridges soon became the order of the day. In the late 1830s and early 1840s, two bridges were built across the Androscoggin, but they did not endure long before their destruction by floods. Finally, in 1869, a two-lane covered toll bridge was constructed and would serve the public until 1927, when it was replaced by a steel open-truss bridge.

Education beyond the grammar school level began to be increasingly of interest to many early Bethel families who wanted their children to have expanded educational opportunities. Although many rural families in an agricultural society depended upon children to help with farm work, sometimes to the detriment of school attendance, New England's Puritan tradition, with its strong emphasis on education, was also at work in Bethel. Ten of the thirteen individuals who were responsible for the creation of Bethel High School in 1835, and would also become its trustees, lived either on Broad or Church Street. They not only had a civic interest in the school, but nine of the thirteen also had a personal incentive: a total of twenty offspring who would become students in the newly created institution. The first board of trustees, with their occupations, included the following: Robbins Brown, president, tanner; William Frye, secretary, attorney; Robert Chapman, treasurer, merchant; Jedediah Burbank, hotel proprietor;

Christopher Bean's ferry between East Bethel and Hanover, circa 1905.

Bethel's Androscoggin River covered bridge had two lanes and was completed in 1869.

Timothy Chapman, farmer; Jesse Cross, miller; Eleazer Ellingwood, shoemaker; Reverend Charles Frost, Congregational minister; John Harris, trader; John Hastings, blacksmith; Jonathan Abbott Russell, schoolmaster; Joseph Sanborn, farmer; James Walker, trader and millwright.

With the arrival of Nathaniel Tuckerman True—who would later become a medical doctor turned educator but at that time was a student at Bowdoin College—as principal, the school was in capable hands. True would later become one of the great promoters of Bethel and a lifelong champion of education. In 1835, he served as the first and only principal of Bethel High School in the district schoolhouse on Broad Street. It began as a modest effort, but soon grew to the point that the school was moved to a hall in the new Bethel House. The following year it became Bethel Academy, since that course seemed the most prudent and economically advantageous in response to a law passed in 1823 by the Maine legislature. In the fall of 1836, a new school building on Church Street, which cost $1,389.46 to build and equip, was opened. This fledgling institution continued to grow and gained a significant boost in 1842, when it received a bequest from the estate of the Reverend Daniel Gould, the town's first settled minister, if the nascent

The main classroom building at Gould Academy, circa 1900. It was replaced in the 1930s by the stately brick Hanscom Hall, a gift of William Bingham II.

institution would change its name to Gould's Academy. This name was in use until about 1922, when the possessive was dropped. Possibly as much as several thousand dollars were supposed to have been willed to the struggling institution, but irregularities in the settlement of the estate resulted in only $832 actually coming from Reverend Gould's bequest.

Perhaps the single most important event that had major implications for Bethel and the whole western Maine region was the arrival of railroad service to the town, which came in March 1851 with the Atlantic and St. Lawrence Railroad train from Portland. This service made it possible for visitors to come to Bethel from great distances with relative ease. In fact, in the next decade, inns and rooming houses began to multiply at Bethel Hill and farmers started taking in summer boarders. Shipping lumber and other wood products from mills built along the tracks to many points in the state and beyond also began to be common practice. A casualty of this demographic change was the loss of population and importance of Middle Intervale, since it would soon no longer be the central village of the town as people began to cluster at Bethel Hill and West Bethel villages. Eva Bean, in her *East Bethel Road*, records the story of the arrival of the first train at Bethel, which attracted much excitement. As the locomotive came around the bend below the village at Bethel Hill, Robert Chapman, a prominent local businessman who headed up the day's program, yelled, "Touch her off Phinn." Due to nervous trembling, Phineas Frost did not succeed in setting off his small cannon, much to the lifelong disgust of Augustus M. Carter (1840–1923), who, although a boy of ten, expected a deafening volley, which "would have done honor to the momentous occasion."

The 1850s were years of growth largely due to the railroad's arrival, particularly at Bethel Hill, where Ira Crocker Kimball (1815–1866), merchant and businessman, had built behind the newly constructed Universalist Church (1853) an attractive enclave of modest houses around a nearly square green that bears his name today. Robert Chapman, another entrepreneur, completed a three-story brick block in 1859 at the corner of Main and Broad Streets, believed at the time by several observers to be the tallest brick building in Oxford County.

The railroad's arrival also brought a variety of visitors to Bethel, including artists who were soon taken with the town's majestic setting of mountains and intervales located on the eastern fringe of the White Moutains. Often identified with the White Mountain School, these artists created picturesque landscapes that were often similar in subject matter and style. Among these artists were David Johnson (*Scene at Bethel, Maine, 1866*), Samuel W. Griggs

Bethel Railroad Depot, built in 1865, as it appeared in the 1890s. *Courtesy of Arlan Jodrey*.

Grand Trunk Railroad wreck, 1901, between Bethel Hill and South Bethel.

Visitors arriving at the Bethel railroad depot, circa 1910.

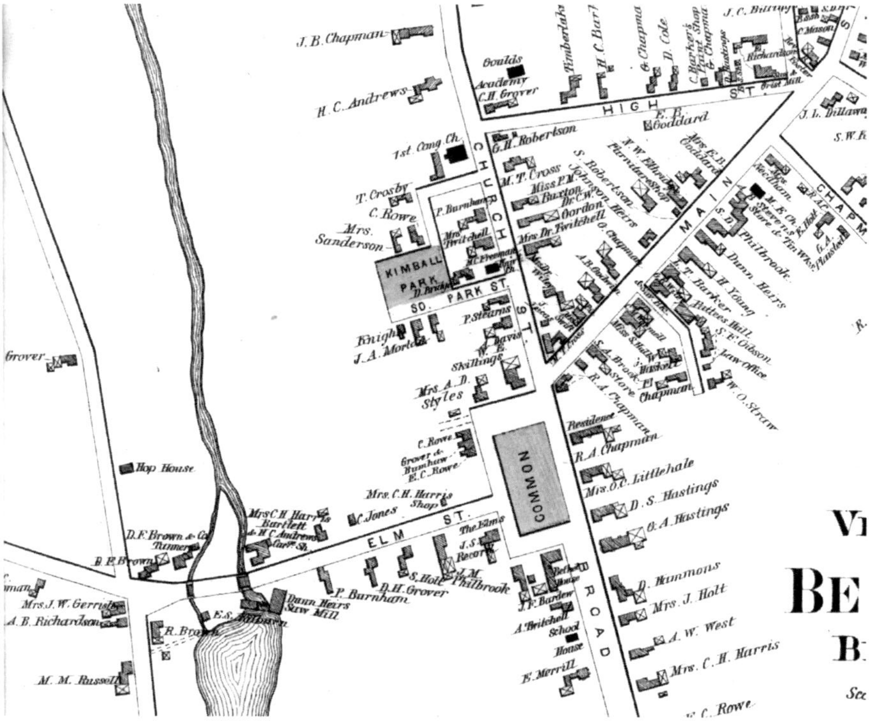

Map of Bethel Hill village from Caldwell and Halfpenny's 1880 *Atlas of Oxford County, Maine*.

(*Meadows and Mountains at Bethel*), Harrison Bird Brown (*On the Androscoggin*), Aaron Draper Shattuck (*Sunset at Bethel, 1860*) and others who continued to frequent the Bethel area into the twentieth century.

Thomas Starr King (1824–1864), who, along with Dr. True, wrote about Bethel for a wider audience, possessed a special fondness for the town's scenic vistas. A well-known Unitarian clergyman and orator, he became famous for his descriptions of the beauties of the American landscape. Credited with naming Bethel's "Paradise Hill," with its sweeping views of the surrounding countryside, he expressed in his highly popular 1859 volume *The White Hills* the hope that "before many years" there would be "a large overflowing from the regular track into the more lonely areas and side chapels of the grand cathedral district." Then, he added, "the wonder will be that Bethel was not from the first more celebrated."

Another significant development in the 1850s was the organization by Dr. N.T. True of what has been cited by agricultural historian Clarence Day as "the first farmer's club in Maine." This club was formed on December

Summer guests at Lovejoy's Hotel on the Bethel Hill Common, circa 1910. *Author's collection.*

22, 1853. True, who was then principal of Gould's Academy and would later become agricultural editor of the *Maine Farmer*, established routines for the organization, which would spread throughout the state and become an important precedent for the Maine Grange, an organization for farm families that would eventually supersede them. The Bethel Farmer's Club usually met twice a month during the winter at members' homes. Although both women and men attended, they assembled separately. Men discussed agricultural topics while women held what might be considered a more informal gathering in another part of the house. Usually apples were the main refreshment for the evening, although sometimes an entire meal was served by the women. Most clubs had about forty members, and there was a one-dollar initiation fee charged. These organizations helped immensely in moving Maine agriculture increasingly toward farming based on scientific principles rather than the outdated ways of one's forefathers.

There is little evidence that the Bethel Farmer's Club continued after the organization of three subordinate granges in the town in the mid-1870s. Bethel Grange #56 was established first at Bethel Hill on November 13, 1874, and was soon followed by Alder River #145 on March 21, 1875 (actually organized in Greenwood by East Bethel folks who later held meetings in that community), and Pleasant Valley #136 at West Bethel on March 29, 1875. Alder River would become dormant in the early 1890s but was reorganized in 1904 and built a hall in East Bethel near Bean's Corner in 1905.

Grange Fair at Pleasant Valley Grange #136 at West Bethel, circa 1920s.

Threshing scene at Bean's Corner, East Bethel, circa 1900.

As early as 1857, it is clear that the Bethel Farmer's Club sponsored a local agricultural fair and exhibit. Agricultural fairs in Maine extend back to 1819, when the Somerset Agricultural Society held a fair in Norridgewock. By 1832, the state began to pay stipends for cattle shows and fairs whose purpose was to promote friendly competition among farmers while adopting better agricultural methods and practices. From 1859 to 1890, when the Bethel fair was held, the exhibition part of the event took place in Pattee's Hall at Bethel Hill. Where the trotting and riding events were carried on, however, is not known. A surviving poster for the Bethel Town Fair of 1872 provides some information on events and people involved, but not a great deal of historical data is available for other years. By 1890, Riverside Park Association was founded, and a new fairgrounds across from Riverside Cemetery offered a trotting track on land leased from Moses A. Mason. When the former Congregational church closed in 1887 upon the death of its longtime minister, Reverend David Garland, it was used as an exhibit hall. This fair continued until 1934, when the depressed economy ended its existence. The facilities remained in neglected condition for some time after the end of the fair. Eventually, the judges' stand near the grandstand was

Riverside Park (Bethel fairgrounds) trotting track, circa 1895.

Interior view of Dr. Nathaniel Tuckerman True's home at the south end of Broad Street, 1880s.

moved to Paradise Hill to be used as an observation post during World War II. Today, the former W.R. Chapman barn that was moved by Henry Boyker up the North Road near the racetrack, which today borders on the present Bethel Airport lot, remains as the only surviving legacy of that bygone era.

Just prior to the Civil War, the town's first newspaper, the *Bethel Courier*, was founded in December 1858. Established by Cady and Smith, a partnership of which little is known, the paper lasted until July 1861. The second issue featured the first installment of a series on the town's history by Dr. True, who as Bethel's first major historian collected considerable and highly significant data on the early years of the region's development and some of its major historical figures, including Molly Ockett. True also served as editor of this fledgling publication for most of its history while leading Gould's Academy as its venerable principal. After his resignation as editor in July 1861, only one issue of the *Courier* appeared, and the subscription list was transferred to another weekly newspaper.

Woodbury & Purington Store, lower Main Street, Bethel Hill, circa 1900.

By 1860, Bethel's population stood at 2,523; according to the federal census of that year, it was the second largest town (next to Paris) in Oxford County. It could boast 474 households with an average size of 5 persons, plus four vacant buildings. The median age of those living in the town in 1860 was twenty-six, with a variety of occupations represented. Not surprisingly, however, over 80 percent of the populace derived their livelihood from agriculture. Due to the arrival of the railroad, by the late 1860s, commercial activity and manufacturing began to increase significantly in the town, particularly in the Skillingston section, at West Bethel and at South Bethel (Walker's Mills). In 1860, 87 percent of the town's citizens were born in Maine. Most of the others had been born in neighboring states, but several were natives of Ireland, perhaps having remained in Bethel after their work in building the railroad.

From the census, it can be determined that twenty-seven households were counted as among the wealthiest citizens of the town, with real estate holdings totaling $5,000 or more. In 1860, the town had one dentist, five doctors, twenty-eight teachers, eight clergymen, three lawyers and a wide variety of skilled and semiskilled workers. Thirteen were listed in 1860 as employed by the Grand Trunk. Two sailors were also enumerated, as was one horse jockey. For a small town in an inland location, this was an impressive number of skills and professions represented, but nothing close to the diversity that would be evident forty years later at the beginning of the twentieth century.

The 1860 election provides some definite indication of the diversity of political sentiment in Bethel on the slavery issue, despite the fact that a son of Oxford County (Hannibal Hamlin, born in 1809 at Paris Hill) was on the Republican ticket with Abraham Lincoln. The Lincoln-Hamlin "team" stood for no further extension of slavery and won the town's endorsement with 206 votes in its favor. The Stephen A. Douglas–Herschel V. Johnson Democratic ticket, which supported non-intervention with slaveholding, garnered 101 votes. The Breckinridge Democrats endorsed locally by attorney and former U.S. congressman David Hammons (1814–1901) supported slavery in the territories and attracted 40 votes. The slate of John Bell and Edward Everett, condemning sectional parties and upholding "the constitution of the country, the Union of the States and the influence of law," received no support in Bethel.

Throughout the Civil War, Bethel voters favored candidates by comfortable margins. By 1864, Lincoln, running with Andrew Johnson of Tennessee on

Bethel-area logging camp scene, circa 1890.

a National Union ticket, garnered 268 votes in Bethel compared with 208 for the Democratic slate of George B. McClellen and George H. Pendleton, a much closer vote than was usually the case. There may have been several reasons for this result, but Lincoln's change in running mate seems likely to have caused some local resentment by his dropping "Maine's favorite son," Hamlin, from the ticket.

Shortly after the firing on Fort Sumter in April 1861, the call went out for seventy-five thousand volunteers to protect the national capital. Maine was asked to furnish one regiment and Oxford County one company. There was only one military unit in the county at that time, the Norway Light Infantry, which at once volunteered and requested additional men to fill up its ranks. Bethel almost immediately sent eight men to join the Norway Infantry to fight what the Republican-leaning *Oxford Democrat* termed "the putrid venom of secession." The Bethel men who went to Norway were described by editor and Gould's Academy principal Dr. Nathaniel True in the *Bethel Courier* as "fine, athletic, noble-looking fellows." They were Solon Robertson, Alfred True (son of Dr. True), A.E. Seavey, Charles P. Stearns, Edward P. Stearns, H. Dolloff, Adelbert Grover and Timothy M. Bean. Before leaving Bethel, they were reported to have made the rounds to bid "adieu" to family and friends. At the railroad depot, where they were to depart for service, a Gould's Academy student, E.M. Wight, mounted a carload of wood and made a patriotic speech that Dr. True described in his column as "appropriate and acceptable" for the occasion.

By the end of May, the eight Bethel soldiers were in Portland and reported to be "in good spirits," according to an account in the *Courier*. They were "eager to get into active service" and had all taken the pledge to abstain from intoxicating liquor, undoubtedly as the result of the many efforts of the temperance forces led by Neal Dow of Portland. A former resident of Bethel's neighboring town, Newry, then living in Portland, presented the Bethel soldiers with various necessities, and a farmer in West Bethel provided them with milk and apples.

In Bethel, what the *Courier* termed "a fine flagstaff" was placed on the town common, symbolizing the town's commitment to the war effort. A company of home guards was organized in May 1861 by Gideon A. Hastings (1821–1905). Hastings, grandson of a founder of Bethel and later the leading spirit in the extensive Hastings Lumber Company operations on Wild River, near Gilead, became in the fall of 1861 captain of Company A, Twelfth Maine Volunteers. During the war, he was promoted to major and was present at the capture of New Orleans, serving in all the campaigns in the Gulf

Major Gideon A. Hastings, a prominent Civil War veteran, founded the Wild River Lumber Company in nearby Batchelder's Grant.

Department. He also participated in the Shenandoah Valley under General Sheridan and after the war became provost marshal of west Georgia and detailed to the Freedman's Bureau. Always a Democrat in politics, upon his return to Bethel after the war, he served as town clerk, selectman, county commissioner and representative to the legislature.

Despite what turned out to be a distinguished record and impressive role for Hastings during the war, a letter to Governor Israel Washburn in October 1861 was not so reassuring. C.J. Talbot of Portland apparently was no admirer of Hastings and his brother-in-law, William K. Kimball of Paris, who also compiled an outstanding war record. Talbot wrote that the two men did "not care about the principle" of the war and would certainly "sell out to Jeff Davis if it found that to be the best." He further accused Hastings and Kimball of being "Peace Men" and "Dana Men" with no "heart for the war." The reference to Dana was John W. Dana, who was the "copperhead" (to those supporting the Union cause, this was the epitome of disloyalty) candidate for governor of Maine in 1861 and received a substantial share of the Democratic support of Bethel, 129 votes. In closing, Talbot urged Governor Washburn to deny Hastings and Kimball commissions on the grounds that "the public will sustain you in standing up firmly and refusing to commission them." The governor was apparently not moved by these pleas, as both men received their commissions.

In July 1861, the Battle of Bull Run resulted in a complete rout of Union forces. Newspaper coverage urged those back home not to lose hope with this loss despite the fact that the Fifth Maine, commanded by Bethel's own Clark Edwards with many Bethel soldiers, was "all cut up." Later it was determined that no Bethel soldier had been lost, but one had been wounded. In addition, the captain's water boy, thirteen-year-old Charles Freeman from Bethel, was missing. Later it was determined that he had been captured and was incarcerated in Richmond. He did not remain a captive very long before he was released in a prisoner exchange and returned to Bethel.

Much of what we know about the effect of the war upon Bethel is found in the period newspapers of the era. Reports of wounds and deaths were often described in detail as they happened and could not have helped but have had an effect upon those on the homefront, especially when the numbers who attended funerals for dead soldiers are considered. Twenty-eight Bethel men died in the war, and their funerals were frequently characterized with sermons strongly supporting the Union cause.

Even more poignant were the reports of returned soldiers who survived the war in Southern prisons. One such example was Peter T. Bean of the Sixteenth Maine, who was captured and spent nearly a year in the notorious Libby Prison. He described an ordeal where he was "glad to get a lean dog to eat." His clothes were all worn off below the waist and his survival was in part due to his ability to stand for long periods of time, as he "did not want to lie down among the filth and vermin."

As grim as the war news was to read in some instances, there are indications that Bethel was indeed becoming increasingly prosperous as the war progressed. By the middle of 1863, the *Oxford Democrat* was reporting that the steam mill recently established west of Bethel Hill appeared "destined to do a good business." Summer visitors seemed to be increasing each year, as additional facilities were being built to house them. Prosperity even extended to the farmer, since Dr. True, always a keen observer of agricultural developments and, as previously mentioned, founder of Maine's first Farmer's Club in Bethel, noted the high prices that farmers were getting for crops, particularly for hops. As the war wore on, consumer prices rose and the Bethel newspaper columns occasionally complained of the high prices paid for goods and services in the town.

The second year of the war brought more reports of wartime activities in the newspapers. Injuries, deaths and near misses were among the subjects that were discussed on a regular basis. On the Fourth of July, Dr. Moses Mason hosted military processions in his grove, where the Declaration of Independence was read by A.S. Twitchell. Later that day, the citizens of Bethel adjourned to the Congregational church, at which a "fervent" Union speech was heard. In the evening, fireworks were set off in West Bethel.

As the summer continued, recruiting offices were set up in Bethel with A.P. Knight as recruiting officer. Toward the end of July 1862, more than one hundred men had enlisted. Fervor for the Union cause reached a new level of intensity that month when General Oliver Otis Howard (1830–1909), recovering from war wounds, addressed a group of local soldiers from the porch of the newly constructed Chandler House. Attending were men from the West Bethel and East Bethel companies. Later, many citizens gathered at Pattee's Hall on Spring Street for a meeting chaired by Dr. True, where Reverend David Garland offered a prayer for the safety of the Bethel soldiers. General Howard also addressed this gathering, making a stirring Union speech, and praised the efforts of the Bethel soldiers on the Potomac. Colonel Clark Edwards was selected for special commendation and cheers were heard for the Union, the Bethel soldiers, President Lincoln and General McClellan. Seven citizens were selected from the meeting to assist the Sanitary Commission in meeting the needs of the war (blankets, clothing, bandages, etc.), with D.F. Brown chosen as chairman.

Many communities on the local level established organizations to assist with the national effort. In Bethel, the Ladies Union Aid Society, founded in 1861, fulfilled this role. Even before the Aid Society was formed, Bethel citizens had sent $185 in cash contributions and twenty-nine barrels of vegetables and two of dried apples to the Sanitary Commission. The Union Aid Society also sent $413 that it had collected. It usually met weekly at Pattee's Hall, but occasionally at a member's home, and it was composed of some fifty women, several of whom had husbands in the war. In an effort to assist in meeting the needs of the men in the war zone, the society sent food and supplies to Portland by train for delivery to the commission in Washington. A typical shipment might include the following, which is recorded in the secretary's minutes for October 28, 1862: one bed sack, four hope pillows, twelve pillow slips, one vest, eight cravats, two pairs of socks, five cotton shirts, ninety-nine handkerchiefs, ten pairs of slippers, fifteen towels, one roll of linen, two and a half pounds of lint, two yards of bandages, one bag of bags, one bag of dried apples, one bag of dried blueberries, four packages of compresses and one bag of beef tallow. Most work was done by hand, but in June 1862, the minutes recorded that "two ladies came in with sewing machines, aiding greatly in forwarding the work of making shirts and drawers." The Ladies Union Aid Society was perhaps one of the best indicators of sentiment for the war effort. These industrious ladies certainly produced large volumes of supplies and not an insignificant amount of cash for the times to support the Union cause.

Another good indication of sentiment during the war years was pure democracy itself, as expressed in town meeting votes. As it still is in many New England communities, the regular annual meeting was held in March, but other special meetings were called throughout the year to deal with wartime issues. In July 1862, for example, a special meeting was held to authorize the selectmen to borrow $1,500 to pay the bounty for soldiers and care for their families. Apparently, this action appeared too generous to some citizens, for in September 1862, it was voted on a motion by Mighill Mason to "pay a bounty to volunteers of twenty dollars and five dollars a month for the first six months." The $1,500 raised earlier in the year was reduced to $900.

The following year, the town voted to raise $2,000 for families of volunteers. A special town meeting in July 1863 resulted in the passing over of an article to pay bounties to drafted men and conscripts. Discussion on this question was "very animated," according to one witness. In August of the same year, those who had opposed passing over the article lost again by a vote of seventy-four to sixteen, but in a second meeting later in the day won approval to provide bounties of $50 each, and the selectmen were instructed to borrow money for this purpose if necessary.

By 1864, the draft had been instituted, and it was voted at town meeting to establish a recruiting committee of Israel G. Kimball (1826–1893),

Gilman L. Blake (1820–1907) and Timothy Bean, with $1,000 to be paid for bounties. Apparently not enough recruits came forward, so a special meeting in December named I.G. Kimball as agent "to procure either enlisted men or substitutes to fill the town's quotas." The town treasurer was authorized to borrow $3,000 for this purpose. By 1865, the last year of the conflict, and with the end in sight, the town, without extensive debate, raised $1,500 to aid the families and volunteers. It appears throughout the war years that as far as town meetings were concerned, there was no broad consensus as to how best to support Bethel soldiers and their families.

Morale is always important in wartime, and the newspapers of the period often urged those back home to remember the men in the war. One paper urged the citizens to write to their soldiers for "many a rough cheek has been wet with tears when a letter has been received from home and who by their letters gave a pledge they were not forgotten." A Bethel soldier, Simeon Sanborn (1832–1892) of the Fifth Maine, wrote his mother from Virginia in December 1861 that he had "some footings, mitten gloves and quite a number of other things sent to me so I am not in any particular want at present." He also reported that he received "about all the Maine papers" and "it was a good thing to have friends especially when you are in the army." Later, Sanborn wrote to his folks in Bethel assuring them that "Old Jeff [Davis] has not gotten me yet." He went on to describe eating lots of fresh fruit, having a good place to camp and getting to "drink whiskey twice a day if we want." On the latter matter, he added, "I don't draw my ration very often and I think if the rest of the boys did not draw so much of theirs, it would be better for them."

Occasionally, deserters returned to Bethel and attempts were made to apprehend them, but few, according to newspaper accounts of the era, proved successful. Bounty jumpers also sought to pass through the town on their way to Canada. At least two were arrested in December 1864, so it is clear enforcement officials were called periodically to keep law breakers in check.

Probably no event of this time has more human interest than the case of Sergeant John Cooper. His story was certainly repeated dozens of times throughout the country. He was reported killed and buried following the Battle of Cedar Creek. By the fall of 1864, he had returned to Bethel to read (much to the joy of his family) his own obituary.

In summary, the Civil War years were significant to Bethel for they marked the greater industrialization of the town, the growth of the summer tourist trade—with many hotels and boardinghouses being established throughout the municipality—and the increased importance of Bethel Hill as a commercial center. It is obvious that in Bethel, as in the North in general, not everyone agreed with the conduct of the war or how those who went off to fight it should be compensated. There were many differences of opinion reflected in town meetings, election results and the activities, for example, of town agent Samuel F. Gibson, an attorney who ran as a "copperhead" candidate for Oxford County clerk of courts in 1863. Later, he would be involved in the Greenback movement in Oxford County.

Undoubtedly, the most important result of the war upon Bethel was its effect on the town's loyal sons. By examining the 1870 census records, it can be determined that five years after the war ended, only 53 of the approximately 180 soldiers whom the town had sent to war were still Bethel residents. Besides those killed in the hostilities, a few died in the intervening years, but apparently for 100 of the survivors, other locations (sometimes distant from Maine) appeared more promising for earning a living and raising a family.

Kimball Park, with houses spaced about a grassy common off Church Street, was the creation of Ira Crocker Kimball (1816–1866). *Courtesy of Rosalind Rowe Chapman.*

In the years after the Civil War, Bethel continued to evolve, but the population began to decline from its wartime high as those interested in agricultural pursuits moved to the West or journeyed to cities to find jobs in factories. In 1870, the census counted 2,268; other later counts were 2,077 in 1880, 2,209 in 1890 and 1,835 in 1900.

One of the cultural highlights of the 1870s was the centenary celebration of the town's settlement in 1774. At a meeting in the Congregational church at Bethel Hill on July 14, 1874, Major Abernathy Grover was selected as chairman and Richard Frye, an attorney, as secretary to organize a "worthy" commemoration. It was voted to hold the celebration on August 26, 1874, with a committee on arrangements appointed to make the necessary plans. This committee included Dr. True, Honorable Robert A. Chapman, David F. Brown (1812–1883), Richard A. Frye (1828–1900) and Moses T. Cross (1811–1887). These members were authorized to make additions to their number if necessary. At a meeting of the committee on July 18, it was voted to invite Dr. True to deliver the historical address and that the dinner should be a basket picnic. Each school district was to be consulted to procure table accommodations.

During the celebration on August 26, bells were rung at sunrise and picnic tables set up on and around the West Parish Common. Many of the private residences at Bethel Hill were "gaily trimmed with evergreens and other decorations." A large American flag "floated across the street between the Bethel House and the residence of Major G.A. Hastings." Major Hastings led the procession that marched later in the morning and included, among others, hunters and trappers; pioneers with axes bearing a banner of birch bark inscribed "Sudbury Canada, 1774"; men breaking and swinging flax; a man pounding corn with an Indian pestle; Twitchell descendants in a carriage; an old mowing machine; a mail carrier on a horse; an old-time doctor riding a horse with his saddlebags; a military band; town officials; and ordinary citizens from many parts of the town.

Seven years later, the centenary of what has come to be known as "New England's last Indian raid" was commemorated in August 1881. Once more, the planning for this event centered on Dr. True; other leaders were Addison Herrick (1847–1932), Dr. Frances Tuell (1847–1925), Goodwin R. Wiley (1846–1911) and Alfred True (1844–1914).

A mock Indian attack group was organized, with Major Gideon Hastings leading the parade, followed by pioneers in costume and citizens dressed as Indians. Contrary to historical fact, a blockhouse was erected on the common and burned. Dr. True delivered another historical address and a

The Indian Raid Centennial historical address was delivered in 1881 at Kimball Park by Dr. Nathaniel Tuckerman True.

dance was held at Pattee's Hall on Spring Street. Estimates of crowds at the height of this event were between three and four thousand.

Finally, one of the great issues of the 1870s was the Greenback movement, which was a national phenomenon with implications for towns in Oxford County such as Bethel. It was part of the legacy of agrarian resistance to capital control and exploitation, extending back to the days of Shays' Rebellion in the 1780s. In some cases, it pitted East against West, conservative against radical, capitalist against farmer debtor. It can be characterized by mercantile and financial groups opposing agricultural interests as well as wealth in land versus those seeking outlets in commerce and industry. Following the "panic of 1873," there was much economic dislocation, with farmers receiving low prices for their produce and facing economic ruin. All this political turmoil temporarily upset Republican domination of the state of Maine, but in Bethel, the Greenback vote, while large, never superseded that of the Grand Old Party. By the early 1880s, prosperity had returned to some extent, and with it came the end of agrarian discontent in Maine and in much of the nation.

Chapter Two

THE WATERSHED YEARS

By the 1880s, developments that would transform Bethel from its eighteenth- and nineteenth-century past began to emerge during a period that historians have termed the "watershed years." One of the first examples of this new thinking and resulting local development followed a special town meeting in July 1886, when $5,000 was appropriated for the construction of a building by the Town of Bethel. This structure would be leased to an entrepreneur with the goal of creating additional employment in the municipality. The building, which could be considered an experiment in municipal socialism, came to be known as the Bethel Chair Factory and provided employment from the mid-1880s until 1912, when the business entered into bankruptcy. The town also added $3,000 to purchase a boiler, engine and machinery for making Shaker chairs in October 1886. J.H. Barrows leased the property from the town at a fee of 7 percent per annum. References to the Chair Factory operations (in 1890 the name was changed to Bethel Manufacturing Company) in local newspapers were made throughout this period, and for a time the town seemed to be regulated by the whistle that sounded each weekday morning for workers to begin operations. After Barrows's bankruptcy, Howard Thurston purchased the property and later his son, Hugh, ran a dowel mill here until it burned down in 1944.

Prior to this time, other milestones had occurred in the town that would shape its future. Two of the most significant for their permanence in determining Bethel's destiny were the creation of the Bethel Savings Bank in 1872 and the founding of the Bethel Library seven years later, in 1879. The Bethel Savings Bank was organized on May 22, 1872, with Oliver H. Mason as president and Enoch Foster as treasurer-secretary. The first year there was

$10,046 in deposits and the first mortgage was for $425. The president's salary was $50 and the treasurer-secretary received $200 in compensation.

The Bethel Library came into being in the winter of 1878–79, when a number of local ladies, including Annie Frye, who would become the longtime secretary of the Bethel Library Association, decided that they should form their own organization. The women, who had been borrowing books from the Mercantile Library in Portland, were becoming increasingly distressed by the difficulties of sending books back and forth over what seemed a long distance. To raise money, a concert and a series of lectures, including one by Dr. True, were held. These efforts raised over $100. On April 14, 1879, at a meeting in the Bethel House, the Library Association was formed with Annie Cross as president and, as a good omen for the future of this organization, Agnes Hastings Straw as treasurer. Originally, the library was located in the Rowe Block, which once stood at what is now the entrance to the Bethel Fire Station. Mrs. Straw also served as librarian. It was a private association with about one hundred members. There were dues charged, and nonmembers could borrow for a fee. The holdings included seventy-nine books by the end of the first year. The location changed several times until 1899, when the library was moved to the former law office of Enoch Foster on Broad Street. This property was later acquired by Agnes Hastings Straw and her husband William O. Straw, who lived in the present Robinson House next door. Upon the death of Mrs. Straw in 1923, the former Foster law office building and a limited amount of surrounding land was willed to the Library Association for permanent use as the town library.

In addition to these major advances, the creation of the Bethel Steam Mill Company during the Civil War was believed to be one of the first of its kind to be run by steam. W.E. Skillings assumed control of the company in 1869. During the next several decades, the firm witnessed expansion in scope and production. W.E. and J.P. Skillings became partners in 1885 and continued until 1890, when the business was sold to the American Bobbin, Spool and Shuttle Company, which failed the following year. J.P. Skillings then took charge of the Steam Mill plant. By 1904, the J.P. Skillings Spool Company consisted of one large spool factory that included a steam plant, four dry kilns, a dye house, a storage shed, a stable, a general store, eight cottages and a boardinghouse.

With all this discussion of mills and manufacturing, it may be surprising to point out that some townspeople did not consider Bethel a mill town. For example, Abernathy Grover in his "Centennial Address" of 1874 insisted that Bethel "is not a manufacturing town." Dr. William B. Lapham in his *History of Bethel*, published in 1891, largely ignores manufacturing.

Enoch Foster's law office (left), later the Bethel Library, and the O'Neil Robinson House (right), Broad Street, circa 1910. *Author's collection.*

In addition, there is an unidentified quote in a special edition of the *Bethel News* published in 1904 with this commentary on the town: "Still it is not in the modern sense, a manufacturing village. There is no foreign element gathered on its outskirts, no hideous row of corporation tenements, filthy from overcrowding, no sharp contrasts between poverty and wealth."

More evidence of the transition in this era taking place in many towns and small cities throughout the nation was the increasing introduction of municipal facilities and services. There was a growing emphasis upon becoming "modern," a term subject to interpretation, but nonetheless a movement that was developing as significant transformations were made throughout the nation. One of the first indicators of this trend was the arrival of wooden sidewalks in Bethel in the 1860s and 1870s. These were later replaced with concrete and granite curbing. In addition, by the 1870s the newspapers began to report on streets being lit with kerosene lamps, tended each evening by a lamplighter. The lamps never gave much light but encouraged citizens to believe that their town was indeed holding the "light" of progress.

Merrill-Springer Mill, near the railroad depot, circa 1900. This was the first source of electric power for Bethel.

By 1890, the Bethel correspondent for the *Oxford Advertiser*, the famed trapper and hunter Joshua G. Rich (1820–1897), boasted that "Bethel is booming these days" and that it had "something of the appearance of a new western town that grows like a mushroom." He cited a building boom and the beginnings of a water system to support his optimism, among other factors. Other indicators included the installation of a sewer system, the consolidation of the district schools with the building of the brick grammar school in 1893–94, the numbering of houses on Bethel Hill, the formation of the Village Corporation and the creation of a volunteer fire department. Progress was indeed coming to Bethel, and by the first decade of the twentieth century the town appeared in almost every sense a thoroughly progressive community and was proud of it.

That impression of progress was bolstered by the selection of one of Bethel's most revered citizens, Clark S. Edwards (1824–1903), as a Maine commissioner to the 1893 World's Columbian Exposition in Chicago. A distinguished Civil War veteran and the Democratic candidate for governor of Maine in 1886, Edwards was tapped by Governor Edwin Burleigh to represent Maine's role in America's tribute to progress. Edwards's appointment created such enthusiasm for the exposition that the local papers were filled with the identities of Bethel people wishing to travel to Chicago in order to experience "the urban industrial wonders of the modern age."

Two other very significant changes during this era were the appearance of the telephone and electric power. The origins of the telephone in Bethel extend back to the 1890s, with the appearance of the first telephone wires on Main Street on July 19, 1895. Prior to the formation of the Bethel Telephone Company in 1903 with $5,000 in capital stock, there were several small groups attempting to provide service. With the arrival of the Bethel Telephone Company, a central office for telephone service was established in 1905 in the Cole Block. Completed in 1891, it was one of the large public buildings that came into being during this "watershed" period. From there, the telephone extended along "farm lines," such as the Middle Intervale Telephone Company (founded in 1904) and the Northwest Bethel Telephone Company (established in 1906), into the countryside. This was made possible from the proceeds of shares of stock that were sold to finance these enterprises. One can only imagine what this change meant to isolated farm families throughout the town and region. Electric power for Bethel Hill

Bethel Fire Department on Mechanic Street during the 1896 centennial celebration parade.

did not come until about 1909, when a power plant was built at Springer's Mill just below the railroad tracks a short distance west of the depot. Rural areas of the town would have to wait, in some instances, until the late 1920s before the power lines were extended to these more remote homes and farms.

Not much is known about the Bethel Fire Department until after the introduction of a municipal water system in 1890. At that time, the first units of a firefighting force, and their equipment, consisted of a hook and ladder carriage manned by twelve men and two hose companies with twelve men assigned to the operation of each hose cart. The department then was composed of thirty-six men and a chief. A new fire station was built in 1965 on the site of the previous one, but it later proved inadequate to house all the equipment and was razed. In 2004, a new fire station set back from the location of the previous one was dedicated.

Also associated with this watershed period was a "police" presence of some kind, as well as (in Bethel's case) a "jail" and a quasi-legal system for disposing of local criminal cases. In 1890, the Town of Bethel appropriated $500 to build a lockup, which exceeded its authorized spending level by $85.75.

A new Bethel Fire Station was dedicated in 2004.

Here miscreants of various sorts as well as homeless souls, often referred to disparagingly as "tramps," were kept in custody and usually fed before being sent away on a morning train. The lockup was frequently referred to humorously as "Hotel Barker," after Henry C. Barker (1842–1924), the turnkey. Some lawbreakers were also brought here by Constable Leander T. Barker (1828–1911) to appear before the local magistrate, Justice Albert Grover (1841–1908), who dispensed "Bethel justice" with a firm gavel.

One more significant development in this transition period was the founding of a weekly newspaper, the *Bethel News*, by Aked Ellingwood of Milan, New Hampshire, at the printing facility he established in the rear of the Cole Block on Main Street. The following year, Ernest C. Bowler of Palermo, who also was the local superintendent of schools, acquired a half interest in the enterprise. In 1897, Bowler assumed full control of the newspaper. Nine years later, in 1906, Bowler opened an office in Rumford and produced the *Rumford Citizen*. This paper was operated separately from the *News*, but they were both printed in the Bethel plant. In May 1908, the two papers were consolidated under the name *Oxford County Citizen*, which has evolved into today's *Bethel Citizen*.

Publisher Ernest Bowler and his wife (left), with employees of the *Bethel News*, circa 1900. *Courtesy of Lee-Ann Wright.*

Closely allied with the newspaper business in Bethel is the evolution of photography. The first known photographer in Bethel was J.E. Small, whose advertisement appeared in the *Bethel Courier* in 1859. No other information seems to be available on him, including the location of his studio or the duration of his stay in town. In the early 1890s, C.S. York was the local photographer. Again very little is known about him except that his studio was located at 29 Main Street and he advertised regularly in the *Bethel News*. In November 1895, York sold his studio and business to Irving Kimball of East Bethel. York stayed on at the studio until January 1896. Kimball was born in 1875, attended Gould's Academy and graduated in 1895. He started his photography business before his graduation, working out of his parents' home until his purchase of the York studio.

From the beginning, Kimball was very active in his business. He was commissioned to take pictures of Gould's Academy for the school catalogue. He also started providing photos to the *Bethel News* and soon became its official photographer. Kimball placed large advertisements in the paper every week and he even provided photographs in one of the *News*' contests. His business became so successful that his sister Rose began to serve as his assistant. Kimball took many photographs of the Bethel area and its prominent citizens for the centennial observance in June 1896. A short biographical sketch on Kimball appeared in this issue as well.

Business was seemingly not as good as the newspaper made it out to be, for by December 1896, Kimball had closed his studio and accepted a job in Waterville, Maine. He left Bethel in January 1897 after marrying a woman also from East Bethel, May L. Holt.

The following year, Kimball moved to Boston to work for Partridge Studios. Two years later, he founded his own studio in Brookline, Massachusetts, where he photographed (among many others) President Calvin Coolidge. During these years, he attended the Massachusetts Institute of Technology, where he was an honor student. Always interested in scientific matters, he became an inventor, serving as vice-president and research engineer for Globe Technolian of Reading, Massachusetts, while still operating his studio. He was forced to retire in 1933 following a train accident, and two years later he came back to East Bethel to reside with his mother-in-law. Following a stroke in 1936, he died and is buried in the Holt lot at East Bethel Cemetery.

Bethel did not remain without a photographer long after Kimball's departure in 1896. R.W. Glidden soon leased Kimball's studio and took over his business. Glidden arrived in Bethel to assist Kimball, but did not stay long.

Irving Kimball (1875–1936) was an outstanding photographer in Bethel in the 1890s and the early twentieth century.

The next proprietor on Main Street was Wilfred Bowler, the brother of E.C. Bowler, owner-publisher of the *Bethel News*. Wilfred Bowler was soon as active as Kimball had been. He advertised heavily and offered many special bargains at this studio. He also sold Kodak cameras. In early 1900, he sold his shop to I.S. Hammond of Lewiston, who hired H.B. Wright to run the Bethel studio for him. In June 1901, the studio was sold to Eugene C. Vandenkerchoven, who was the photographer until February 1908, when he developed tuberculosis and moved to the Hebron Sanitarium for treatment. W.L. Merrill of Norway leased the studio while Vandenkerchoven was in Hebron. S.A. Parsons was the Bethel photographer during the years of the First World War. Little is known of him since he did not remain very long in the town.

During the 1930s, Frank A. Goddard took the photos for the Indian raid sesquicentennial. A native of Quebec, he worked for the Canadian National Railway in addition to maintaining his photography business.

Lawrence Lord was active as a photographer in Bethel from 1942 to 1950. He and his wife also had an orchestra that became well known in the area.

Probably the best known of the more recent photographers was Donald S. Brown (1919–1996), who started a photography studio on Main Street following his return from World War II and his graduation from the New York Institute of Photography in 1946. For a time he also was at the Cole Block, but later he moved to his home on Chapman Street. In the mid-1950s, he joined his father's business at Citizen Printers and became the news photographer for the business until his retirement in 1985. His son Kurt briefly had a studio at the family home here prior to moving to Westbrook, where he has been involved in the photographic business for many years.

A municipal water system appeared to be the vision of four men: William E. Skillings, Judge Enoch Foster, Gideon A. Hastings and Samuel D. Philbrook. In 1888, they brought Albert Stanwood—an engineer from Waterford, Maine, with Boston connections—who conceived of a system that would send water by gravity from Chapman Brook, on the north side of the Androscoggin, to a reservoir on Paradise Hill and then by gravity to households and businesses in Bethel Hill village. This effort was organized in 1889 as the Bethel Water Company with eight corporators; by the following year it was fully operational, with Enoch Foster serving as president. About one hundred Italian immigrant workers housed in barracks near the Androscoggin bridge were brought in to dig the trenches for water pipes. John J. Moore of Hingham, Massachusetts, was the general supervisor of construction. It took some eighty carloads of pipe

Before the advent of the automobile, nearly all Bethel residents kept horses. *Author's collection.*

weighing over two hundred tons for the project. The shipping bill paid to the Grand Trunk Railway was $1,500, the largest amount up to that time ever collected at the Bethel Depot. A.P. Jenness, superintendent of the Fryeburg Water District, oversaw the building of the sixty- by ten-foot dam on Chapman Brook, which was constructed by Benjamin R. Bryant. (It was this structure that was destroyed in July 2007 by a severe rainstorm.) The first water from Chapman Brook flowed into the village on September 26, 1890, and served twenty-five hydrants for fire protection. Will Garey was the first Water Company superintendent.

The arrival of a public water system, however, made it more urgent for the town to install a sewer system to ensure proper drainage and prevent the spread of disease. In light of this concern, annual town reports in the latter half of the 1890s began to publish the observations and recommendations of the Bethel health officer, C.D. Hill, MD, who, in addition to detailing cases of contagious disease, began to urge the installation of a sewer system to eliminate what was referred to euphemistically as "those nuisances." By 1898, the town had begun to provide public sewerage beginning on Broad

Street, continuing down Church Street to Park Street, where it was directed down to Mill Brook and from there flowed to the Androscoggin River. Dr. Hill urged the expansion of this system to include other parts of Bethel Hill, especially Main Street, which took several years to achieve, for, as he ended his 1902 report, "There cannot be any mistake in appropriating money for the preservation of public health."

During these transitional years, the town paused long enough in 1896 to celebrate the centenary of its incorporation. This appeared to have been a casual affair, unlike the previous celebratory occasions in Bethel past, such as those held in 1874 and 1881. Captain R.B. Grover of Brockton, Massachusetts, seems to have been the catalyst for initiating this milestone in the town's history by sending a generous donation to the Bethel selectmen, who responded by appointing a committee of prominent men, including Judge Enoch Woodbury, Major Gideon Hastings, Samuel B. Twitchell, Israel G. Kimball, John Barker, T.H. Chapman, Eldridge C. Wheeler and E.C. Bean. Various committees were created, including Procession, Reception, Decoration, Entertainment, Antiquarian and Invitations.

On the big day, a triumphal arch was erected at the foot of Broad Street. On one side, there was a sign reading "Welcome to Our Guests" and on the reverse, "Home Sweet Home." Houses and businesses were elaborately decorated, most in patriotic red, white and blue. In a corner of the Cole Block, displays of antiques and curiosities were featured, including the gun Dr. Moses Mason's father used at the Battle of Bennington and a map of the Magalloway River drawn by Dr. Mason on birch bark. Once more, Major Gideon Hastings led the parade and was described by the *Oxford Democrat* as appearing, despite his seventy-five years, with "all the lustiness of youth." The parade featured Chandler's Military and Bryant Pond Cadets band. Also participating were a large number of bicycles, the Bethel Fire Department, Brown Post of the Grand Army of the Republic with cannons, the Bethel Police, students and the Goddess of Liberty, merchant floats, Indians, rangers and carriages of guests and the press (including Holman Day, reporting for the *Lewiston Journal*). Following the parade, it was reported that three thousand people enjoyed a bean supper at a hall on Main Street, where several activities were featured, including the recital of a poem about Bethel by Mary C. Herrick. In addition, a merry-go-round was set up near the newly dedicated Odd Fellows Hall (constructed in 1890) that was a major attraction during the festivities. In summing up the observance, the *Bethel News* proclaimed that "a happier or more orderly throng of people never trod the streets of our town than on this occasion." More impressive in the paper's view, however, was the observation that there was "no sign of intoxication to mar the pleasures of the day." Neal Dow, Maine's leading temperance advocate, would have been proud of this sterling example of behavior on the town's special day.

At this point, it may be instructive to briefly review the history of the Bethel Hill Common in the West Parish to see how it fits into the transformative process suggested by this watershed period of the town's past. It begins with Eleazer Twitchell, mentioned earlier as a figure in the Indian raid of 1781. He once owned all of what is today Bethel Hill. He built a house, known as "the Castle," close to the present site of the Opera House Condominiums. In 1797, he gave the lot near his home to the West Parish for use as a common. Although this gift was not recorded in writing, he did so with two conditions: (1) that the plot be cleared of stumps and rocks, and (2) that the Congregational church be built upon it. Neither condition was met, so Twitchell took his land back, fenced it and reputedly used it as a wheat and potato field. Despite this decision, he remained a moving spirit in the development of the West Parish and was eventually persuaded to take down his fence to provide a parade ground for the militia. At approximately the same time, Broad Street was opened and made extra wide for muster marches. Twitchell died on June 23, 1819, and his heirs subsequently deeded the common to the West Parish on April 24, 1823.

From this time until the Civil War, not a great deal is known about the Bethel Hill Common. Fourth of July celebrations were annual events, but these were usually held at the center of the town, Middle Intervale in the East Parish on the common in front of the meetinghouse or in Dr. Mason's grove in back of his house in the West Parish. During the Civil War, Dr. N.T. True drilled the Bethel Zouaves on the Bethel Hill Common, but apparently this was still not a very pleasant spot to be. In his 1874 "Centennial Address," True lamented the condition of the common and expressed the hope that "the ladies of the village will derive means to have the rocks removed and the surface graded."

Dr. True's plea went unheard until a meeting was called at the Bethel House on April 28, 1878, when a group of prominent citizens organized an effort to beautify and improve the Bethel Hill Common. By May 14, 1878, the *Oxford Democrat* was reporting that the common was "cleared of stones and graded under the supervision of William E. Skillings." The *Democrat* also recorded that the common was to be enclosed and "made attractive by the transplanting of trees, erecting seats and laying out gravel walks."

The Indian Raid Centennial observance was held on the Bethel Hill Common on August 3, 1881. According to a detailed account in the *Oxford*

Rowe's Store was built in 1884. Ideal Hall, on the second floor, was once the center of Bethel's cultural events. *Courtesy of Nancy Stickney.*

IDEAL HALL
EDWIN C. ROWE

Bethel Hill Common was enclosed with a wooden fence when this photo was taken about 1890. *Author's collection.*

Democrat on August 9, 1881, a blockhouse was built that was attacked by the "Indians." The pageant took liberties with the historic record, as the common was not known to have been the site of the original hostilities.

From a surviving photograph of the 1881 Indian raid festivities, it is possible to determine that a fence was in place around the common and that the grading had taken place. One of the purposes of forming the Village Corporation in 1889 was a desire to improve the common. So far as is known, that remained the state of things until about 1900, when Dr. John Gehring and his wife, Marian True Gehring, began to take an active interest in the common, overseeing the planting of a wide variety of shrubs and plants. During this time, the common became a park-like haven of lush foliage, in sharp contrast to its earlier, stark appearance. In addition, Mrs. Gehring and the Columbian Club, a women's literary organization, became the leading spirits in placing an appropriate fountain on the common in November 1902, which was long an attraction until its removal in 1980 because of its alleged deteriorated state. In 1902, they raised $645 for the fountain and landscaping. Two years later, another $125 was raised for shrubbery, grading and the creation of flowerbeds. By the 1930s, the common had been returned to an elm-shaded, park-like space with few of the bushes and shrubs that had marked the Gehring era.

Mention has been made of a number of major buildings constructed during the late nineteenth and early twentieth centuries. Probably no structure proved as essential to the town as the Cole Block, built in 1891 by two brothers, Fred and Elmer Cole, of East Bethel. They commissioned one of Maine's best-known architects, George Coombs of Lewiston, to design a building that was originally planned to be brick and to be built in East Bethel (possibly with bricks from Edson Bartlett's brickyard there). It is not known why the Cole brothers changed the building's location to Bethel Hill, but it can be deduced that they chose wood over brick simply for economic reasons. Much excitement was created in Bethel by the construction of such a large structure, but soon after its completion the brothers were unable to pay the mortgage. The building then became the property of the holder of the mortgage, the Bethel Savings Bank, which owned the building until it was transferred to the Town of Bethel in 1982.

During the period from the 1890s to the 1950s, the Cole Block was a center of commercial, social and civic activity on Bethel Hill. On the first floor in front was a space occupied by a millinery store, later a jewelry store and finally a bank until the Town of Bethel took over this space for the town office in 1968. The Bethel Savings Bank and the Bethel National Bank were also on the first floor on the other side of the center stairway leading to Odeon Hall. After the bank moved out, real estate offices were here until the town took over and the Bethel police was assigned this space. Farther back, with a side entrance, were long the offices of Addison E. Herrick and Ellery C. Park. Toward the rear of the building, there was once a reading room until taken over by the *Bethel News* and its successor, the *Citizen.* On the second floor overlooking Main Street from the 1890s until 1968 were the municipal offices. When the town manager form of government took effect in 1954, it was also the office of the town manager. In addition, there was another law office on the second floor in the 1940s.

At the top of the stairs is the entrance to Odeon Hall, believed to be so named by Joan Stearns Kilborn after her world tour in 1907. For generations, the hall was the center of the town's social, political, cultural and, for some, religious life. With a balcony and seating for over five hundred, it was the site of Gould's Academy graduations, countless dances, plays, socials, minstrel shows, concerts, lectures, Chatauquas, movies (both silent and "the talkies"), town meetings, political caucuses and (in the 1960s) Roman Catholic religious services. Due to William Rogers Chapman's influence, Metropolitan opera star Geraldine Farrar once sang there. Other figures of national and international significance who have made appearances here include Jane Addams, of Hull House fame and the recipient (along

Cole Block, with Odeon Hall, dates from 1891. It was long a significant cultural center and remains the site of town government.

with Nicholas Murray Butler of Columbia University) of the 1931 Nobel Peace Prize; in 1910, Addams delivered a lecture on her settlement house experience in Chicago.

For years, Harvey Bragdon used the hall for a theatre for silent movies. Pianists for these films included Doris Lord and Beryl Morgan. He later introduced "the talkies" to Bethel. Among the projectionists were Ray Crockett, Clayton Crockett, Arthur Morgan and Fred McMillin. As a teenager, Ashby Tibbetts worked for Bragdon announcing films and posting notices of forthcoming attractions. The movie era ended for Odeon Hall in 1940, when Max Zallen opened a new modern theatre with a marquee farther down Main Street. In the 1930s, many Bethel residents watched breathlessly as a man billed as the "Human Fly" scaled the full height of the building by crawling up the façade. The Cole Block was listed in the National Register of Historic Places in April 1998.

Within its borders, Bethel has a least fifteen graveyards or cemeteries: Abbott Family, Bartlett, Bird Hill, Chadbourne Family, Chandler Hill, East Bethel, Flat Road, Grover Hill, Middle Intervale, Mount Will, Pine Grove,

Riverside, Stanley Family, Walker's Mills and Woodland. In her book *East Bethel Road*, Eva Bean cites other possible gravesites, including one at the foot of Blake Hill (within sight of Route 26), one on Holt Hill in East Bethel and one below Bean's Corner at East Bethel, the so-called "Peary Cemetery." No one is certain who is buried in these likely gravesites. The Peary Cemetery, for example, contains a number of depressions enclosed by an impressive stone wall. Prior to 1843, the Hanover Cemetery would also have been included in this list of Bethel cemeteries.

When the first cemetery or graveyard was established in Bethel is unknown. Certainly Grover Hill at the Steam Mill or Skillingston section of the town and Bartlett at East Bethel are among the town's earliest burial sites, although Riverside also contains several eighteenth-century graves. Many of the first graves were likely marked with wooden markers, which have long since disappeared. A number of graves were later marked with something more permanent, often fieldstones with names and dates crudely chiseled into them, or perhaps a slate stone with more decorative names preserved in fine lettering. Slate stones are found in a number of Bethel cemeteries, but the later marble markers are far more numerous and appear highly susceptible to one of the ravages of modern life—acid rain, which in some cases has all but eradicated inscriptions. Granite markers, which seem to be impervious to industrial pollution, began to gain popularity in the late

Herrick Bros. Co. Garage, lower Main Street, circa 1910. It was an early dealer in automobiles and their repair.

nineteenth century, and this continues to be the predominant stone used today in most Bethel cemeteries. In addition, there are a few "metal stones" in several cemeteries as well as unusual ones such as those using boulders and quartz crystal.

In summary, the watershed years were transformational for Bethel, moving it from the age of the horse in 1880 to the automobile by 1903, when William W. Hastings became the first person in Bethel to own an automobile. In fact, the *Bethel News* warned the citizens of the town to be aware of his reputation as "a reckless driver of horses and horse-drawn teams and carriages." Such a figure clearly had a "foot in each era," but it was now certain that he, like his hometown, was headed boldly toward the future, not mired in the past.

CHAPTER THREE

THE ERA OF GEHRING, HANSCOM, CHAPMAN AND BINGHAM

The decades from the mid-1890s until the mid-1950s might be called the era of Gehring, Hanscom, Chapman and Bingham, since these four men in many and profound ways left their mark on the town's character and development. Dr. John George Gehring (1857–1932) and his wife Marian True Gehring (1850–1936) were commanding figures in Bethel from 1896, when Dr. Gehring established his clinic at the end of Broad Street for persons with nervous disorders, until failing health made it necessary for him to retire in about 1925. William Rogers Chapman (1855–1935) was an outstanding musical conductor who also composed and led choruses and orchestras in a variety of locations. In 1897, with the assistance of Mrs. Gehring's and his wife's superb organizational skills, Chapman founded the Maine Music Festival, which became a major musical presence in Maine and other parts of the Northeast until the arrival of radio in the 1920s caused the festival's popularity to fade. (The last festival occurred in 1926.) Also arriving in Bethel in 1897 was Frank Edward Hanscom (1863–1940), who became principal of a struggling Gould's Academy, which, aside from Dr. True, had never had a head of school stay much more than a year or two. In fact, by the time Hanscom assumed the principal's position at Gould, there had been over thirty-five predecessors. Hanscom would serve in this post for nearly forty remarkable years, during which time the modern Gould campus began to take shape. Finally, William Bingham II (1879–1955), who arrived in Bethel from Cleveland, Ohio, in 1911 to seek relief from what appeared to be—in the language of the period—"nervous disorders," would decide to become a permanent resident and through his independent wealth significantly change the character and landscape of the town.

Dr. John G. Gehring established a clinic for the treatment of persons with nervous disorders in Bethel in the 1890s.

John George Gehring, who would later be known as "the wizard of the Androscoggin valley," was born in Cleveland, Ohio, the second of four children, on the Fourth of July 1857, the son of Karl August and Wilhelmina Gehring, who were German immigrants. Gehring's father, a shrewd grocer in Cleveland, although a man of modest means, was able to send his son to Western Reserve University (now Case Western Reserve University), where he earned a medical degree in 1885, joined a practice after his graduation and also served as a lecturer at what is today the College of Wooster. Later, Gehring experienced some kind of mental breakdown and visited the Southwest in an attempt to restore his health. While there, he met a Boston couple, George and Marian Farnsworth, who befriended him, and he followed them back to Boston, where George Farnsworth died in April 1887 and was subsequently buried in Woodland Cemetery in Bethel, his wife's hometown. The following year, in October 1888, John G. Gehring

OFFICIAL SOUVENIR PROGRAMME

FIRST ANNUAL FESTIVAL

AUDITORIUM,

BANGOR, OCTOBER 14, 15, 16.

PORTLAND, OCTOBER 18, 19, 20.

1897.

WILLIAM R. CHAPMAN,

DIRECTOR-IN-CHIEF.

ORCHESTRA OF SEVENTY MUSICIANS.

CHORUS OF ONE THOUSAND VOICES.

PUBLISHED BY THE MANAGEMENT

PRICE, FIFTY CENTS.

Lakeside Press, Printers and Engravers, Portland, Me.

The title page of the first program of the Maine Music Festival, founded in 1897 by William Rogers Chapman of Bethel. *Author's collection.*

Frank Edward Hanscom was an outstanding Gould's Academy principal from 1897 to 1936.

Philanthropist and Bethel summer resident William Bingham II (1879–1955) was at one time believed to be the wealthiest man in Maine. *Payne Archives.*

and Marian True Farnsworth (Dr. N.T. True's daughter) were married. She was seven years his senior and the mother of one son, George B. Farnsworth Jr., who would also become a medical doctor and, as the stepson of Gehring, succeed him in managing the affairs of William Bingham II.

Mrs. Gehring inherited her father's home at the end of Broad Street following his death in 1887, the same year her husband died. She and Dr. Gehring spent considerable time in Europe, where, among other accomplishments, the doctor received a doctor of science degree from the University of Berlin. A Portland physician, Dr. Frederick H. Gerrish (1845–1920), was likely also instrumental in Gehring's training for operating the clinic he later founded in 1896. Gerrish relied on hypnotism as one of his strategies for treating mental disorders, and his influence can be found in the regimens that Gehring employed in the nearly thirty years that the clinic existed.

Dr. Gehring received a medical license to practice in Maine in 1895. The following year, Dr. True's former homestead burned while the Gehrings were in Portland, and a new home was built later in 1896 farther back on the large lot that graced the end of Broad Street. The first patients (although that word was discouraged and replaced with "guests") were largely from

Dr. Gehring's "guests" sawing and splitting wood as part of their therapy for relieving nervous disorders.

Harvard, giving Bethel the distinction of being referred to as "the resting place of Harvard University." Later, the New York society people would come, and then a national clientele. "Guests" attending Dr. Gehring's clinic were encouraged to balance rest with vigorous exercise. At times, hypnotism was used and intestinal regularity was carefully monitored by this "doctor of body and soul," who achieved international renown with his techniques. The Gehrings were also very active in the Bethel community. Dr. Gehring was a founder of the Bethel National Bank in 1905 and was long the vice-president and later the president of the Gould's Academy Board of Trustees. He was also awarded honorary degrees from Bates College in Lewiston, Maine, and Rollins College in Winter Park, Florida, where he and his wife sometimes wintered.

Frank Edward Hanscom was born in West Poland, Maine, in 1863 to a farm family. His mother died when he was seventeen and his education was disrupted for a time. He later received encouragement from the superintendent of the schools, Bert Fernald, who later went on to become Maine's governor. Fernald encouraged Hanscom to teach at a small district school, where the money he earned was used to attend Hebron Academy, from which he finally graduated at the age of twenty-two as valedictorian of his class. From this distinction, Hanscom became superintendent of schools and a teacher in Mechanic Falls and Poland; he also served as principal at

Oxford High School for six years before coming to Gould's Academy at the age of thirty-four. His appointment was likely influenced by Ellery C. Park, a Bethel attorney, who would later serve on the Gould Board of Trustees. Park and Hanscom attended Hebron Academy together one class apart and had become friends during those years. Hanscom assumed the leadership of a struggling academy, but it was his leadership in working closely with Dr. Gehring and his wife that would, in time, bring the academy back to the glory days when Mrs. Gehring's father had headed the school.

William Rogers Chapman was born in Hanover, Massachusetts, where his father, the Reverend William Rogers Chapman, was temporarily located. He had previously been pastor of several Congregational churches in Boston. Left fatherless at the age of three months and christened on his father's coffin, William Rogers Chapman spent his boyhood in Bethel, which his ancestor, Reverend Eliphaz Chapman, had named in 1796. Here he attended Gould's

Gould's Academy women's basketball team, circa 1900. *Author's collection.*

Academy briefly before his mother's marriage to William J. Valentine of New York City. The family then moved to Fordham, New York, where the young Chapman's education was continued at the School of the Collegiate Dutch Reformed Church. Here he prepared for the ministry, as this was his father's request. However, he showed so much musical talent that his studies were soon diverted to music. After studying music with some of the greatest teachers in the United States, he was sent to Leipsic and Berlin to further his musical training. Upon his return to the United States, he became the organist in a large church in New York City. He also received, simultaneously, an appointment as a teacher of vocal music in the New York public schools, where he established a powerful presence. In addition to his school and church duties, he also founded and conducted the Musurgia Society of male voices, the Apollo Club of male voices and the Rubinstein Club of women's voices, as well as the Metropolitan Club of mixed voices. It was during this period that he began to give periodic concerts in the Metropolitan Opera House, which were great successes. This led to the organization and direction, by 1897, of musical festivals in northern New England and New York, as well as New Brunswick. Under his direction, these festivals featured community choruses, organized throughout the region, which attained an international reputation for their excellence and attracted some of the world's greatest

William Rogers Chapman and his wife in their sleigh on Main Street, circa 1910.

artists and orchestras. Chapman was later honored by the University of Maine with an honorary doctor of music—the first person provided this distinction by that university. He married the former Emma Louise Faulkner of Chicago and they had one daughter.

The last major figure to be discussed in this chapter is William Bingham II, who was born in Cleveland in 1879. Bingham's family was of English ancestry and had lived in Connecticut for four generations before twenty-year-old William Bingham departed from the Nutmeg State to Cleveland, Ohio, to become a successful businessman, banker and, for a time, politician, serving as a state senator. This William Bingham was the grandfather of William Bingham II, whose father was Charles William Bingham, a member of the Yale College Class of 1868. He married the daughter of U.S. senator Henry B. Payne and they produced five children, three boys and two girls. William Bingham II was the second oldest and grew up with his siblings on Euclid Avenue's "Millionaire's Row" in Cleveland, where he was privately tutored during his early years and attended University School. As a seventeen-year-old junior, he was sent to St. Paul's School in Concord, New Hampshire. The year 1896–97 was to be the last of his formal schooling, for a combination of typhoid fever, the loss of his mother and beloved older brother, Oliver, and a sense of deep loneliness led him to travel restlessly, often with a young doctor as a companion. Among the locales he spent time in during this period of his life were several winters in Santa Barbara, California, one winter in a Nova Scotia logging camp (where he reputedly entertained the lumbermen with his violin) and a lengthy period of horseback riding in and around Jackson Hole, Wyoming.

Through his Cleveland connections, he undoubtedly heard of Dr. Gehring's regimen in Bethel, and in 1911 he traveled to the clinic with another Cleveland friend, William J. Upson. They both seemed to find some relief from their nervous disorders under Dr. Gehring's care and decided to settle in Bethel, and for a time were business partners. Bingham was fairly social during his early years in Bethel, but when a Boston newspaper published an article in 1925 that announced that the wealthiest man in Maine lived in Bethel, everything changed. This fact was further emphasized when it was announced in 1932 that Bethel took first place as "the richest town in Maine" based on deposits in the Bethel Savings Bank. For the rest of his life, Bingham lived in seclusion, dealing with the world only through his doctors, nurses and other trusted associates.

Bingham's family was wealthy but became even more prosperous following the death of his uncle, Oliver Hazard Payne, in 1917. Payne was born in

Cleveland in 1839 and never married. He attended Yale, left to serve in the Civil War and was wounded at Chickamaugua, but returned to lead troops and was commissioned a colonel while in his mid-twenties. After the war, Colonel Payne returned to Cleveland, where he joined his brother Nathan in the oil business just before John D. Rockefeller, who had gone to high school with Oliver, started Standard Oil. The Payne brothers' oil interests were later merged with those of Rockefeller. After the merger, Payne served as treasurer of Standard Oil, where he received credit for making Rockefeller rich. He later left Standard Oil with large stock holdings and went on to found the American Tobacco Company, the Great Northern Paper Company and the Tennessee Coal and Iron Company. He also was heavily involved in railroad development. He later owned the *Aphrodite*, the largest steam yacht in the United States, which sailed the world. He gave millions to help found the Cornell Medical College, and many more millions were donated to Lakeside Hospital in Cleveland, Yale University and the New York Public Library. When he died in 1917 at the age of seventy-eight, he left the bulk of his estate, valued at $179 million, in trusts to two nieces and four nephews, one of those nephews being William Bingham II. It was believed that Colonel Payne was, at the time of his death, the second wealthiest man in the United States after John D. Rockefeller. Colonel Payne was known to be reclusive and was a lifelong bachelor, which may have had some influence upon his nephew's personality and later behavior. In addition, the colonel's generous philanthropic disposition may also have had some bearing upon William Bingham II.

In any case, Bingham appeared to find Bethel a "good fit" and responded well to the attention paid him by the Gehrings. The doctor became a "father figure" for him, and Marian seemed to fill a void left vacant by the death of his mother. Coincidentally, he was elected to the Gould Board of Trustees the same year that his inheritance from his uncle came to him. His first recorded gift to the academy, $2,500, was made that year as well, thanks to Mrs. Gehring's influence in lining up wealthy donors to assist in endowing her father's beloved academy. From that time on, Bingham began to provide generous support to the academy. The first major building he funded was a gymnasium in 1922 bearing his name, followed by a girls' dormitory named for Mrs. Gehring in 1925, a principal's home in 1930, a classroom building in 1933 named for Hanscom, Farnsworth Field House (named for Mrs. Gehring's son, George) in 1940 and, finally, a boys' dormitory named for Liberty Holden (a Gould alumnus, onetime owner of the Cleveland *Plain Dealer* and the academy's first major donor) in 1944.

The year Bingham arrived in Bethel, 1911, was also the year that the Prospect Inn, overlooking the Bethel Hill Common, burned. Two years later, Bingham, along with four other former Gehring patients, opened the Bethel Inn on the site of the old hotel. In the 1920s, he purchased an entire mountainside to protect the Chapman Brook Reservoir, the source of Bethel's water supply, and deeded it to the Bethel Water Company. By 1922, he decided to become a Bethel resident and acquired the Wright Cottage next to the Gehrings on Broad Street. Following renovations, based on plans developed by the architectural firm of Coolidge and Carlson of Boston, the Shingle-style house became his Bethel residence for the remainder of his life. Also during the 1920s, he began the Bingham Scholars program to assist young men and women who were short on funds to get an education. Their names were kept confidential and the recipients never saw him. Applicants dealt initially with Dr. Gehring, then his stepson, Dr. George Farnsworth, and finally with Dr. Arthur Walters. Among the most famous beneficiaries of this assistance was Edmund S. Muskie, whose legal education at Cornell was paid for by Bingham. Bingham had a remarkable memory for detail and could recall hundreds of needy students he had assisted.

Dr. Gehring's health began to decline; he closed the clinic about 1925, and in 1930, Dr. Farnsworth was chosen to help "Will" Bingham handle

Gould's Academy men's basketball team, circa 1905.

Rescuing items from Prospect Hotel, on the Bethel Hill Common, at the time of the 1911 fire.

Completed in 1913, Bethel Inn was largely funded by William Bingham II and designed to house Dr. Gehring's patients.

Bingham Gymnasium, built in 1922, was the first of William Bingham's major building gifts to Gould's Academy.

his affairs. Later, Dr. Walters, a Florida physician, was engaged to care for Bingham since Dr. Farnsworth's expertise was in obstetrics. In 1927, Bingham gave $200,000 to fund an entire hospital ward in Dr. Gehring's honor at the Neurological Institute of New York. Dr. Gehring's illness prompted consideration of ways to improve medical services in rural areas, primarily in Maine. This led to the creation of the Bingham Associates Fund in 1932, which began to support improved medical services in Maine and in the Boston area. The establishment of the Bingham Associates Fund required legal assistance, and Sidney Davidson, a New York attorney, was hired as Bingham's personal lawyer. In 1935, Davidson suggested the creation of the William Bingham II Trust for Charity (known today as the Bingham Trust) with an initial gift of $5,000. The Betterment Fund was established after Bingham's death in 1955, and the William Bingham Foundation from the residue of Will's estate that came to his sister, Elizabeth Blossom. After her death, a portion of her estate was added to the principal of that foundation. One final significant development with Bingham support was the establishment of the Pratt Diagnostic Clinic at Tufts–New England Medical Center, which allowed many Bethel citizens to have free state-of-the-art medical diagnosis and treatment. Bingham's "eyes and ears" on the local scene for this program was Betty Burns Thurston, a retired nurse who made recommendations for medical treatment and sometimes personally drove potential patients to Pratt for their diagnosis and treatment.

Three other men residing in Bethel at this time deserve mention, as they were closely allied with the academy as leading trustees and also were intimately tied to local affairs. Judge Addison E. Herrick was a figure immensely respected in the town. He presided over the academy board for many years, but also served as a state representative, state senator, Oxford County judge of probate and, for a half century, treasurer of the Bethel Savings Bank. His wife, Mary Chase Herrick (1857–1936), a Blue Hill native, was a leading figure in the intellectual life of the town and the aunt of Smith College professor Mary Ellen Chase, well known in this period for her novels with Maine settings.

Eben Kilborn (1846–1940) was a very successful businessman along with being president of the Gould board. His wife, Joan Stearns Kilbourn (1879–1956), was also prominent in town; she published a book, *Over the Horizon*, reflecting on her travels around the world.

Ellery Park (1864–1849), law partner of Judge Herrick, was long on the academy board as treasurer and superintendent of Buildings and Grounds. He was also active in town affairs.

Another Broad Street resident of note in this era was Mary True (1845–1919), Mrs. Gehring's half sister and Dr. True's daughter, who was a famed teacher of the deaf in the Boston area until her retirement. One of her most famous pupils was Mabel Hubbard, who would later marry Alexander Graham Bell. The Bells often called on Miss True in Bethel on the way to their summer home in Nova Scotia.

One of the signal events of this era was the dedication of the Civil War Soldier's Monument in May 1908, which was recorded by the *Bethel Citizen* as "a glorious day" where "every fluttering flag waved patriotism and every heart throbbed with love of country." A parade numbering over four hundred persons included the twenty-five-piece Rumford Falls Band, several speakers, the municipal officers, Civil War veterans, a large group of women, schoolchildren with flags waving, "scarlet-shirted" firemen and, finally, citizens of Bethel and environs. The procession was led by the marshal of the day, Major Adelbert Twitchell of Newark, New Jersey, who was mounted, as were A.S. Chapman and Augustus M. Carter, comrades of his old battery. Also mounted was Fred L. Edwards (1865–1947), son of Colonel Clark S. Edwards of the Fifth Maine. Joining in the group

Winter view of Bethel Hill Common from the belfry of the Kimball Block (fire station), circa 1890. Paradise Hill and Mount Abram are in the background. *Author's collection.*

The great American organ builder Ernest Skinner and his wife, Mabel Hastings Skinner (a Bethel native), are buried in Bethel's Woodland Cemetery. *Author's collection.*

were Ira C. Jordan, A.M. True, T.M. Bean and Brown Post (Grand Army of the Republic) commander A.H. Hutchinson. The procession began at Gould's Academy on Church Street, marched around the common, down Broad Street to Main Street and from there to the monument. The whole village was bedecked in flags and patriotic bunting. At the monument, the veterans and Relief Corps, gathered with schoolchildren, were surrounded by over two thousand citizens. A speakers' stand was erected at the side of the monument, where space was provided for seating the speakers, the clergymen, municipal officers and guests—about twenty in all.

After a musical selection from the band, the Reverend William Curtis of the Bethel Congregational Church led the assemblage in prayer, followed by a patriotic song featuring the schoolchildren, under the leadership of Bessie Andrews. Next came Ellery C. Park, attorney and presiding officer. He paid tribute to the sacrifices of the Civil War soldiers from Bethel and to all those who had made the monument possible.

Brown Post commander A.H. Hutchinson was then summoned for the unveiling of the blue granite soldiers' monument, which was purchased from the Smith Granite Company of Waverly, Rhode Island, for $1,550 through public subscription and town appropriation. Prior to that, he spoke movingly of the Bethel Civil War veterans and their esteemed commander, Colonel Edwards, whose daughter, Nellie Edwards Phipps, was called upon to officially pull the string, causing the flag to drop from the monument as the band struck up the national anthem.

E.C. Bowler, editor of the *Citizen*, was the next speaker and provided a short address on the importance of citizenship in a democratic republic. He was followed by Alfred M. True, who recalled the soldiers of 1861 to '65 and the spirit of those days that stirred the hearts of young men and led them to the front to defend the Union. He remembered some of the Bethel "boys" as "touched by the spirit of the hour and went forward to rank among the bravest and the truest soldiers of that terrible war."

Sarah E. Putnam, a former resident and prominent figure in State and National Women's Relief work, was then introduced and spoke briefly of the work of the Relief Corps. She recounted a number of the instances in which the corps had provided assistance to veterans since its organization in 1883, totaling between $3 and $4 million of relief work.

Major John Mead Gould (1839–1930) of Portland was the next speaker. Having previously distinguished himself as a gifted writer and speaker, he delivered a brief address specially formulated for all the children. Finally, the program ended with the marshal of the event, Major Adelbert Twitchell, giving a very touching valedictory to the old soldiers present and his fellow comrades, which "stirred the hearts of many to tears."

A "camp fire" meeting in the evening at Odeon Hall continued the spirit of patriotism. It had taken over eighteen years since Bethel's Brown Post, Grand Army of the Republic, had first proposed a soldiers' monument to honor the town's Civil War veterans. The post had been lobbying hard for the statue to be placed on the common at Bethel Hill, but this proposal ran into firm opposition from the Gehrings, who, as has been previously cited, controlled this community resource with a self-appointed noblesse oblige that few dared question in an era when deference to power and authority were more likely to prevail. The struggle continued for years until it was finally compromised by placing the monument on a "heater piece" at the corner of Mechanic and Main Streets, then the site of the town's bandstand, which was removed to make way for the impressive statue that endures to this day.

Bethel's Civil War Soldiers' Monument was dedicated on Memorial Day 1908 with elaborate ceremonies.

Not much appears in the local newspapers during World War I, which began in 1914, until after the United States declared war on April 6, 1917. The following week, a patriotic meeting was held in the Universalist church, where efforts to form a Relief Corps and Red Cross were begun. The next week, the *Citizen* reported that "the first demonstration of patriotism was shown" when a group turned out to escort the men who had enlisted to the railroad station. The procession was headed by a fife and drum corps, which formed in front of the post office and concluded "with flags flying, the boys were given a good send off." The first group to enter the service consisted of Gould's Academy students Herbert Bean, Elwin Wilson and Vivian Hutchins, plus others from the town, including Winfield Howe, Asa Burgess, Albert Silver, Leslie Coburn and Vernon Judkins. All of these men joined Company D, which formed at Norway, Maine.

Thus began nearly two years of intense interest in and support for United States participation in the war. Almost immediately, concern for food was established as a priority (with spring planting not far ahead), and a concerted plea was made to local citizens to produce one acre of hoed crops. Many of the town's more prominent men of this era became part of the campaign, including Judge Addison E. Herrick, William Bingham II, Dr. E.L. Brown, Irving Carver (1884–1942), Gilbert Tuell (1854–1918), Fred Merrill (1879–1948), Daniel Hastings (1840–1925), Herbert Rowe (1877–1939), Ellery C. Park, Guy Thurston (1865–1952), William C. Bryant (1877–1950), Ira Jordan and numerous others. Growing more food and food conservation were two causes that received much attention during this period. "This was a time that the home garden became popular," recalled Pearl Ashby Tibbetts (1884–1982), whose husband, Dr. Raymond R. Tibbetts (1875–1958), served in the U.S. Navy at Kittery during the conflict. Eventually there would be a food conservation movement, with 340 Bethel families pledging to restrict their consumption.

Accompanying this emphasis on agriculture were other activities to help the conduct of the war, including joining the Red Cross (open to men and women for a one-dollar membership fee). A room for this purpose was opened over L.W. Ramsell's store on Main Street in the Hastings Block, at the corner of Main and Church Streets. Items such as bandages and sterile dressings were prepared here for overseas shipment. Also working to supply wartime needs was the Navy League, formed in 1903 with clubs throughout the nation to promote a strong naval defense. Both encouraged knitting of articles for the servicemen and were responsible for sending 271 Christmas bags overseas in October 1917.

Financing the war was not neglected in Bethel either. In May 1917, a Liberty Loan Committee was formed to encourage the purchase of war bonds. Attorney Ellery C. Park served as chairman of this drive, with many of the town's most notable men and women serving on the committee and assisting in the sale of these securities. There would eventually be four campaigns between the middle of 1917 and October 1918, with some $400,000 worth sold. Not surprisingly, William Bingham II was listed as one of the leading investors.

By the end of May 1917, the draft became a reality, and in June of that year all male residents between the ages of twenty-one and thirty were required to register. The *Citizen* almost weekly carried announcements of those approved for induction and those rejected. There also were advertisements designed to stir patriotic fervor and motivate the "slackers" to volunteer.

As in most war economies, shortages for the civilian population soon became apparent. "Sugar was scarce, also flour and molasses," recalled Paul B. Head (1898–1980), a World War I veteran whose father, H.N. Head, was then operating the family store in West Bethel. Other commodities were limited, but not to the extent that they would become during World War II.

By the summer of 1918, however, the *Citizen* was warning readers against "Sunday joy rides" in an effort to save precious resources such as gasoline.

One of the sidelights of the American effort was the campaign to protect the American border with Mexico from the raids of Pancho Villa. Albert "Bert" Grover participated in that episode, and several of his letters were published in the *Citizen*. Since much of the work of his unit was involved in preventing incursions from Mexico, his letters provide useful insights. After one skirmish, Grover wrote his mother in Bethel that he expected "more trouble with them [Mexican insurgents] before they find out that they can't have their own way."

There was also other correspondence published from the men in the service, but probably none as poignant as that of George Mundt, who was early sent to France and who would die in the fighting there in July 1918. His letters capture some of the enthusiasm typical of young men who saw themselves as defenders of democracy, but even that noble cause did not diminish a sense of homesickness as Mundt wrote in a letter of November 13, 1917. Here he noted that "the line from Gram brought back memories of Xmas with a pair of gloves always for my Christmas present." Even the mud and rain, which made conditions worse, brought back comparisons with home. "The roads," wrote Mundt, "are just like Brandy Brook hill only more slippery and just as steep in places." Nevertheless, this nostalgia was tempered by such comments as not wishing to return home "till the Stars and Stripes" were "on Kaiser William's flag pole in Berlin."

News of Mundt's death did not reach Bethel until August 1918, when a letter sent by one of his friends, Fred L. Armstrong, arrived in town. Writing to the dead soldier's mother, Armstrong paid tribute to her son as "one of the most reliable, and cool, and steady cannoneers we had." "He was," continued Armstrong, "always full of fun and life, a good comrade, ready to buck into any hard work." The *Citizen* followed the publication of this letter with the comment that "the above letter was received by Mrs. Mundt last week, but she has received no official notice and is hoping the fears are groundless." Curiously, it was not until March 1919 that official word was received from the War Department that Mundt had indeed been killed in France and was buried there.

Accompanying the letter referring to Mundt's death was the news that another Bethel man had been wounded in the left arm and neck by a high explosive shell. Herbert R. Bean survived but carried the scars of combat for the remainder of his life. Mundt's death and Bean's wounding brought home to many in Bethel the grim realities of war.

In addition to the risks of death or maiming that always exist in combat, there was the ever-present danger of pneumonia. Many soldiers stationed both abroad and on the homefront succumbed to its perils. One Bethel man who survived a bout was Winfield Howe, who wrote his mother from France after the crisis had passed in a decidedly upbeat mood: "Well, Ma, don't worry about me at all for I'll be all right pretty soon and ready to talk to Fritz again."

Local efforts to support the "boys," besides the sale of bonds, were perhaps best highlighted by the campaign to knit items that would make life on the warfront more endurable. Sweaters, socks, wristers, mufflers and helmets were in constant demand. William Bingham II and William J. Upson were apparently the chief suppliers of money to buy yarn for these items, and every available woman was encouraged to learn to knit so that Bethel might make a good showing in this endeavor. Contests were conducted and incentives offered to increase participation. One worthy of note was a challenge sponsored by W.J. Upson to see who could knit the most sweaters between October 1917 and Easter 1918. It turned out to be Mrs. W.H. Hutchinson, who produced fifty sweaters during that period.

The first of modern wars produced several additions to the already grim horrors of combat, including poisonous gas. A few Bethel men experienced the effects of this new weapon, but none was believed seriously affected. Those back on the homefront were encouraged to save fruit "stones," which were used to produce carbon that was essential in protecting soldiers from the gas peril.

By October 1918, there were rumors of an impending armistice. When these reports became a reality on November 11, 1918, a sense of jubilation prevailed throughout the United States. The *Citizen* reported on the scene in Bethel: "At twelve o'clock, the pupils of the Academy and Brick School paraded the streets, the bells rang, the whistles blew and about fifty automobiles decorated with flags filled with people made merry for an hour." This was followed by an open air meeting on the Bethel Common.

The following year, at the March 1919 annual town meeting, a committee was appointed to honor veterans of the war. Reverend H.S. Trueman was appointed to serve as chairman, with Ellery C. Park as secretary and Fred A. Tibbetts as treasurer. What emerged from these deliberations was "Our Boys Day," which was held on May 14, 1919. The festivities were highlighted by bright and sunny weather, which greatly enhanced the already hearty enthusiasm for the event and ensured large crowds. Activities began with a Grand Parade, which featured Bethel's only war baby, Frank O'Neil

Maine governor Carl Milliken was the featured speaker at the "Our Boys Day" ceremonies held on the Bethel Hill Common in 1919.

Robertson Jr., a catered luncheon (free to "our boys"), a baseball game between Bethel and Rumford (won by Rumford 6–1) and a variety show at Odeon Hall, where each veteran received an honor certificate. Maine governor Carl L. Milliken was present and addressed the crowd assembled on the common. It was indeed a fitting tribute to those who had served, but even with the end of hostilities there was much relief work to be done.

Bethel residents continued their interest by supporting the Red Cross and the War Work Campaign, which were committed to assisting all those who had been dislocated in Europe by four years of destruction. These actions were but a continuation of the effort that had drawn the support of most organizations and individuals in the town. Bethel had contributed much in a time of great national sacrifice and had done so without hesitation.

Chapter Four

BETHEL AT MID-CENTURY

The Great Depression years of the 1930s had a significant impact on the later history of the nation leading to World War II and the postwar era. Bethel was definitely affected by the economic hardship of the 1930s, but its impact was not as serious as it was in other parts of the nation. Bethel people were relatively fortunate, although at the time some families complained bitterly about their economic plight.

Several things about Bethel played into making this period a less difficult time economically. There had never been large-scale industries here, but instead modest-sized mills and plants rarely employing more than a hundred or so workers. The economy had always been based upon relatively small wood mills, farms and businesses. For generations, one of the town's most important exports, also true of the state, was its young people.

Also playing into the experience was the strong Yankee tradition of thrift, ingenuity and the rock-solid goal of living within one's means. Numerous men possessed the experience of combining a bit of farming, lumbering and odd jobs on a regular basis. For women, there were more limited possibilities, but some worked outside the home in a mill, cleaned houses or did laundry or sewing. In one way or another, these resourceful citizens survived this difficult time because they had several skills and were used to doing a number of jobs.

The Depression did not come on suddenly, but evolved gradually after the stock market crash of October 1929. All during 1930 and 1931, businesses began to close, unemployment rose, many lost their savings and some their homes. By 1932, more than half of the nation's industrial plants were idle. At the same time, there was no safety net—no social security, no food stamps, no insurance for bank deposits. The only relief was emergency aid from local authorities.

From the town reports of this era, a number of observations can be made. As the Depression deepened, there was an increase in the unpaid tax list. By 1934 and 1935, some homes and other property were being seized through foreclosures or tax liens. The percentage of these actions was lower in Bethel than in some parts of the nation, but nonetheless, it was deeply felt by the families affected by this economic catastrophe.

Poor relief, as reported in town reports, went from $713 in 1929 to $2,317 in 1930 and $4,129 in 1932. By 1933, this figure began to decline as New Deal programs started to provide some relief. Another indication of the situation was the number of homeless persons housed at the lockup. In 1931, the number fed totaled 409. This statistic continued to increase until in 1936, it came to 1,112. After 1936, the numbers began to decline as the Works Projects Administration (WPA), the Civilian Conservation Corps (CCC) and other employment-related programs helped ease the plight of those thrown out of work.

Lower tax collections and increased expenditures for the poor placed greater pressure on the town's finances. The selectmen's response was decisive and effective. Wages of town employees were cut in 1933. Laborers on the highways had their pay cut by a dollar a day. Since some of them were previously earning no more than three or four dollars per day, this amounted to a painful loss in wages.

The elementary and grammar school teachers also found their salaries reduced. The town's teachers had never been highly paid in comparison with those in some other Oxford County towns. The highest paid teacher in 1929 was Ethel Bisbee, who earned $900. By 1932, Mrs. Bisbee's pay, and that for all other teachers, had been cut 10 percent, bringing the salaries of the town's educators below county averages. In 1933, the salaries were cut another 10 percent. As miserably low as these salaries were, at least Bethel was able to pay its teachers throughout this decade. In some towns, salaries were not paid for months and "script" or "IOUs" were issued in place of cash during this trying time. Bethel high school students attended Gould Academy, which was heavily subsidized in this era by William Bingham II so that faculty members there felt none of the financial pain that their public school contemporaries endured.

The town remained solvent through this crisis. Both the Bethel Savings Bank and Bethel National Bank proved sound and no savings were lost. In addition, William Bingham kept the Bethel Inn open, and some local people continued to be employed there. His gift of Hanscom Hall to Gould Academy in 1933 also brought a modest number of construction jobs to local workers as well.

Despite the hardships felt by many Bethel people in this period, economic conditions began to improve by the late 1930s. Events that evolved into World War II would soon begin to have their effect on the town and its people.

One of the bright spots in this decade was the 1931 sesquicentennial observance of New England's last Indian raid, which, as previously noted, occurred in 1781. The 1931 event was held on the exact anniversary of the raid on August 3. As in 1881, there was no attempt to convey what really happened during this historic event. A settler's house, erected on what is today the Gould Academy athletic field, was attacked and burned. It was good theatre but nothing like this had actually happened in 1781; however, newspaper coverage boasted that this festivity attracted the largest crowd ever assembled in Bethel, estimated at ten thousand. There was an extraordinary parade with lots of elaborately decorated floats, and a baseball game between Bethel and Lovell (won by Lovell, 11–4). Over three bushels of beans were baked in the ground ("bean-hole-beans" style), one hundred pounds of hot dogs served and fifteen gallons of clams consumed, among other food offerings. One of the highlights of the day was the appearance, courtesy of William Rogers Chapman, of Princess Wa-hoo-ah, singing Indian songs in costume. There were other attractions, including a greased pole competition, which was won by John Twaddle. Toward the end of the day, a large dance floor, specially installed by Dr. S.S. Greenleaf and crew on the common, provided an opportunity to spend a special evening dancing away the cares of the times.

Weather was also a major newsmaker in the 1930s, with the great flood of 1936 superseding those of 1896 and 1927. The Androscoggin rose to the level of the tracks on Railroad Street in Bethel, and there was considerable disruption of services and property damage throughout the state (the $8,000 estimate for Bethel was basically for road repair). In addition, the Hurricane of 1938 caused the loss of numerous trees and timber stands, making it necessary to harvest as soon as possible in order to market the downed trees before insect infestation made them unmarketable.

In 1941, Bethel was a town of 2,034 inhabitants who were emerging from the Depression of the 1930s seemingly with fresh confidence despite the war clouds that had begun to gather in Europe. New businesses were opening and mills that had long been idle or at reduced capacity were hiring workers. Small businesses on Main Street were not so numerous as they had been twenty years earlier, but there still remained a variety of shops where one could buy everything from shoes to ice cream. The town library contained nearly eight thousand volumes, and Gould Academy was in the midst of expanding its

The 4-H float in Bethel's 1931 Indian Raid Sesquicentennial parade, which attracted a large crowd.

Floodwaters in 1936 covered the tracks along Railroad Street. This was the highest level of flooding of any recorded on the Androscoggin.

campus with the addition of new buildings, all gifts of William Bingham II. Carric Wight was the superintendent of the town's public schools. The postmaster at Bethel Hill was Arthur Herrick and at West Bethel was Paul Head. John Butts was the president of the chamber of commerce, and the selectmen, assessors and overseers of the poor were Ernest Bisbee, Carroll Abbott and John Howe. Alice Joy Brooks was town clerk, John Harrington was town treasurer and Walter Bartlett was tax collector.

Reading the columns of the *Citizen* in the early stages of the ever-enlarging conflict, one would scarcely know that Europe had been at war since September 1, 1939. The pages of the local newspaper were filled with news of fraternal orders, sixty-three parties and church events. The Depression of the 1930s had taken some toll on the townspeople, but suffering was not so obvious as it was in other parts of the nation. The value of the town's real estate, however, decreased by nearly $200,000 between 1930 and 1940, so it can be determined solely from a dollar perspective that the Great Depression had exacted a cost in Bethel, to say nothing of the silent suffering of the town's populace. By 1941, the mills had begun to prosper.

Equally significant from an employment standpoint was the fact that quite a number of Bethel people spent the war years in such places as Bath, Portland and South Portland, where there was great demand for labor as well as high wages in the defense industries. Among Bethel people who worked in coastal defense plants were Herbert Rowe, Malcolm Farwell, Ernest Mundt, Malcolm Mundt, Guy Gibbs and Robert Kirk.

All these employment opportunities were good news for many Bethelites whose livelihood depended directly on these economic activities; their effect on others, including shop owners, was more indirectly felt. In September 1939, the war appeared thoroughly remote, with little possibility of its touching the lives of any Bethel person. It was not until the following year that the *Citizen* began to report on events connected with the hostilities in Europe.

Among the first instances of contact with the war were the reports made by Arthur Herrick's daughter Kathryn, who in a series of letters to the editor discussed conditions in wartime London, Paris and other parts of the continent. About the same time, in Bethel, the American Red Cross began a campaign to provide relief following the invasion of the Netherlands, Belgium and Luxembourg in May 1940. A house-to-house canvass for funds, with First Selectman Ernest Bisbee serving as treasurer, attempted to raise $200. In July, the *Citizen* announced that the quota still had not been met, and editor Carl Brown wondered aloud why this was so. Apparently the war was still not of primary concern to many Bethel people. During this period, the *Citizen* began publishing syndicated columns on war preparedness, and Eugene Van Den Kerckhoven, owner of the telephone company and a World War I veteran, led the drive to recruit candidates for the army reserve in Bethel.

By the fall of 1940, a call went out for men ages twenty-one to thirty-six to report at Odeon Hall to register for possible service. Town Clerk Alice Brooks registered some 238 men during the month of October, 100 fewer than had been anticipated but a number that appeared to reflect national percentages. A lottery was announced that would later decide the order of call-up. One further indication of the concern for increased security was the fact that the border patrol was now stationed in Bethel (and it would be for the war's duration) in order to check traffic to the Canadian border.

During early November 1940, the *Citizen* carried Republican Party advertisements appealing to Bethel voters' patriotic sentiments regarding the sacred right to vote and emphasizing how many in Europe were now denied that privilege. GOP candidate Wendell Wilkie handily won Bethel

Hastings-Howe family gathering, East Bethel, circa 1894. Clarence Decatur ("C.D.") Howe is in the center in a white shirt. *Author's collection.*

with 524 votes to 287 for President Roosevelt, and there were two votes for the Communist candidate for president, Earl Bowker.

At the beginning of 1941, Sidney Dyke enlisted in the Royal Canadian Air Force as an instructor. Vernon Brown was drafted into the service on January 23, 1941. In the "East Bethel" column of the *Citizen* appeared news that Clarence Decatur Howe (1886–1960), whose parents were natives of East Bethel, had arrived safely in the United Kingdom after his ship, the *Western Prince*, was torpedoed by a German submarine. Howe, minister of munitions and supply in the Canadian cabinet of Prime Minister William Lyon Mackenzie King, had sent photographs relating to this episode to his uncle, George K. Hastings (1863–1944), in East Bethel. In February 1952, a portrait of Howe would be featured on the cover of *Time* along with an accompanying story on his many accomplishments as a Canadian cabinet minister.

In March 1941, the first group of Bethel draftees was called for service. Its members included A. Lincoln Merrill, Donald S. Brown, Stanley C. Carter, Harris Tyler, Gasta Lantendresse and George A. Parsons. With this announcement, the *Citizen* began printing news of selectees, promotions, transfers, discharges and furloughs.

By May 1941, there appeared in Bethel the first notices for defense bonds and postal savings stamps. During the Memorial Day exercises, Elwood F. Ireland, Gould Academy headmaster, presented the address of the day, stressing the grim world situation and some of the challenges ahead. Also occurring at this time was the first plea for USO funds.

During the summer of 1941, it was announced that a 236-mile oil pipeline between Portland, Maine, and Montreal, Quebec, would be built as a defensive measure. Since it would pass through Bethel, there was much local interest. Described as the largest project to occur in the Bethel area since the building of the Atlantic and St. Lawrence Railroad in the 1850s, the pipeline was completed in the fall of 1941.

In July 1941, the town was stunned by the news that W. Ashby Tibbetts, son of World War I veteran Dr. Raymond Tibbetts, had been killed in Canada, where he had joined the Royal Canadian Air Force. During the funeral service in Bethel, offices and shops were closed in tribute to his memory.

By the summer of 1941, a number of things occurred to bring the war's effects closer to everyone's grasp. A food stamp program was imposed, and the first plea for saving aluminum appeared in the *Citizen*. A column, "This Week in Defense," became a regular feature of the town's weekly newspaper, and army recruiters held sessions each Wednesday afternoon in Odeon Hall.

In the fall, efforts by the American Legion were made to form a home guard. "Captain" Leslie Coburn was selected as commander, and a call was issued for seventeen- to sixty-year-old men to enroll as a measure of preparedness in case the nation should become involved in war. Fifty men were necessary to form a company. By October 1941, this goal had been realized and was followed by the election of officers.

By now, the regulations dealing with the Office of Civilian Defense (OCD) had begun to take shape. The Bethel leadership was undeniably practical so that the excesses that plagued the national effort were not in evidence in the town. Bethel hardware store owner and World War I veteran D. Grover Brooks (1892–1955) headed the town's civil defense program and in December 1941 was also named chief air raid warden. Most of those involved in Bethel's civilian defense program were listened to by their fellow townspeople, in marked contrast to the OCD in Washington, which by 1944 was largely discredited by the American public and Congress.

In October 1944, the American Red Cross appealed for sewing machines to work on shirts to assist with relief work. The following month, the British War Relief Campaign was organized in Bethel. Card parties were held to raise funds, and barrels were placed around Bethel shops to collect items useful to this effort. Yarn was also collected at Allen's Shoe Store on Main Street.

As winter approached, the activities of the home guard intensified. Its members drilled two evenings a week in the upper hose house until the growing numbers forced their move to the former Bethel Grange #56 building (known as Pattee's Hall in the nineteenth century) on Spring Street in December 1941. There were frequent pleas in the *Citizen* for recruits, but with no pay, a physical examination and some expense for inducements, there appeared little to offer recruits except feelings of patriotic pride and a sense of duty. These apparently worked for a time, but until the United States became directly involved in the war, questions arose as to the extent that this patriotic fervor could be maintained.

Waiting for U.S. entry into the war was not to be long, for on December 7, 1941, the Japanese attacked Pearl Harbor. Onboard the USS *Oklahoma* was a Bethel man and 1939 Bowdoin College graduate, Stanley Allen, who was killed and whose name was later (1949) added to the local American Legion Post. Also in the line of fire were the following Bethel men who survived the attack: Christino Onofrio, Willard Thayer and Carl Tucker (Hickham Field), Harold Young and Henry Robertson (Schofield Barracks) and Charles Chapin (Wheeler Field).

Norris Brown was one of many Bethel World War II soldiers.

The next day, the United States Congress declared war on Japan, and the defense effort in Bethel came alive. Almost immediately, a Red Cross drive for $1,200 was on, and the Central Maine Power Company issued a request that there be no holiday streetlighting because of the increased defense load.

At Gould Academy during the war, there were worries about keeping dormitories full, but these proved needless in the end. Gas rationing disrupted sports schedules, but interscholastic competition was not completely abandoned. The track team won the county championship in 1942 and the basketball team achieved the same honors in 1944. In 1943, Gould officials cancelled its entire basketball and winter sports schedule. An aviation school was established at the academy under the leadership of Alfred J. Fortier, and students were active in bond drives, raising $10,000 in bonds and stamps in just one week. Edmond J. Vachon, then a teacher of French at the academy, administered tests for the army and navy to students. Several faculty members left for the service during the war, including Edmond Vachon, George Bowhay, Howard P. Chivers, Robert T. Bateman and Paul Hunsicker. In all, some 370 Gould graduates (18 of them women) served in the armed forces during World War II; 18 of them died in their nation's defense. The *Academy Herald* for this period contains few references to the war, but the catalogue for the same time was more direct in addressing the challenge of the conflict by stressing the need for physically fit students with a "thorough education in the basic secondary education subjects." The catalogue continued to emphasize that it would soon offer training in "such matters of military importance as lend themselves to classroom teaching as navigation, applied mathematics, range finding, radio communication, map making and reading, meteorology, current European and world history, war problems, economics and photography." Finally, the catalogue summed up the academy's emphasis on physical strength, which it declared would "receive more careful emphasis than ever before."

Of all the Gould Academy graduates in the U.S. Army, probably none had as distinguished a career as James D. Alger, Gould class of 1930 and West Point graduate, who was one of the first to go overseas as a lieutenant colonel in charge of a tank battalion. He was in the first battle fought by American forces abroad at Kasserine Pass in North Africa. Taken prisoner there, he spent the better part of the war in a German prisoner-of-war camp. The *Citizen* frequently contained articles referencing the fact that Alger was still in the hands of the Germans.

Central Service Station, Main Street, Bethel, 1930s.

In April 1942, the *Citizen* announced the first shipment of cigarettes from Bethel to servicemen. This one went to Stanley C. Carter (1917–1970), stationed at Shelby, Misssippi. Not surprisingly, long after the war he would die of lung cancer. Later in that month, it was announced that Paul Thurston, prominent Bethel businessman, had been appointed as the Oxford County chairman of Civil Defense.

By May 1942, gas rationing was fully in effect. Sugar consumption was also severely curtailed. Fat was to be turned in to the Legion Hall on Main Street for use in the war effort, and air raid practice signals were announced at this time; ten short rings on the telephone announced an alert, with one long ring providing the all-clear signal.

The following month, 123 people were fingerprinted at Odeon Hall. More veterans were encouraged by the American Legion post in Bethel to join the Legion and to display the flag throughout the duration of the war. Marriage was no longer a barrier for military service. In addition, all enlistments were now extended to the end of hostilities plus six months.

In January 1942, Maine was declared a danger zone because of its proximity to Europe. Civil Defense operations were organized, with some two hundred responding to the leadership of First Selectman Bisbee. A disaster committee was also formed under the direction of dentist Dr. E.L.

Brown (1885–1967), assisted by two grocers, Phillip Burns and Myron C. Bryant (1902–1961), with numerous committees selected to assist this effort. The police were also recruited in support of this campaign, with Frank Hunt (1887–1959) serving as chairman and William S. Hastings (1901–1943) as his assistant.

By February 1943, the *Citizen* was announcing that it was giving free subscriptions to men and women in the service; later discontinued because of the numbers involved, a special subscription rate of one dollar per year was substituted for those in the service. The following month, the town of Bethel voted to raise $1,000 for Civil Defense. The town reports of the war years frequently mentioned the shortage of equipment and parts to keep public services operating smoothly. Also critical was enough manpower to keep the rolls of the fire department full; many men were lost to the Selective Service and the lure of high-paying war-production jobs on the Maine coast.

It was about at this stage of the war that the first blackout trials were made with mixed success, according to the account in the *Citizen*. The use of blackout curtains and the prescribed dimming of automobile lights did not receive universal endorsement, at least in these formative months. Also occurring at this time was the announcement that all twelve-gauge shotguns were now reserved for government use. As a result, the war seriously affected the gun and ammunition business of H.I. Bean (1871–1952) on Spring Street, but he managed to carry it on through the conflict.

Of human interest was an article that appeared in early 1942 in the *Citizen* on Mrs. H.E. Merrill of East Bethel, who had four sons in the service. The patriotic response to the war efforts appeared to be high and growing since the Red Cross had little difficulty raising over $1,200 in a matter of weeks. A paper drive by the Boy Scouts yielded $37.53, and the P.H. Chadbourne children contributed $9 in nickels and dimes to the town's war effort.

Alder River Grange #145 in East Bethel initiated a unique means of raising money for the purchase of defense bonds. It required each member to wear some kind of costume at meetings; those who did not were fined five cents, and this money was dedicated to buying bonds. Farmers in the Bethel area were urged by the Grange and other organizations to support the war effort with Victory production, which often was plagued by shortages of labor and supplies.

By the spring of 1942, air raid wardens were selected, as well as firemen, auxiliary firemen, policemen and messengers. The home guard was soon absorbed by the state guard. Members were still required to furnish their own firearms, but would be paid if called up by the governor.

Wartime propaganda began to appear regularly in the *Citizen* and no doubt in other media as well. One advertisement during this period displayed a Japanese face with the caption, "Wipe the sneer off his face, buy U.S. savings bonds and savings stamps." It was urged that 10 percent of everyone's income be spent on bonds and stamps.

During the summer of 1942, the *Citizen* carried numerous pleas for people to conserve scrap metal and contribute to the drive that was now on. By the fall, some nineteen tons of metal had been collected for the town's war effort and $26,000 worth of war bonds and stamps sold.

Introduced in the middle of 1942 was V-Mail, which brought information (usually on the personal side) to Bethel from fighting men and women. Mail service was unusually important during wartime, bringing news of loved ones to and from the town. One can only speculate on how much a letter from Maine lifted the morale of Bethel's servicemen and women or how much a message from the front reassured anxious ones at home. The *Citizen* carried instructions for anyone writing loved ones in the service not to dwell on the difficulties at home, but to emphasize the positive side of things so as not to add to the cares of those engaged in the defense of the nation.

On a more public side of things was the establishment of an air raid warning station on Paradise Hill (used until the fall of 1942) near today's present Eden Lane and another on the Buck Farm at Middle Intervale. These were manned by many volunteers headed by Gould headmaster Elwood Ireland, who was given the title of chief observer. Participants in these operations received special training in detecting enemy aircraft, a distinctive blue and white armband as well as an observer pin.

Apparently, interest in the operation at Paradise Hill flagged and it did not reopen until February 1943 in a greatly expanded form. The former judges' stand at Riverside Park was donated by Spanish-American War veteran Henry Boyker (1879–1961) to be used as an observation post. It was renovated as a community project of the Bethel Lion's Club and placed near the site of the previous warning tower. On July 4 of the same year, it was dedicated formally to the memory of Stanley Allen, who had been killed earlier at Pearl Harbor. With more than fifty people in attendance, Headmaster Ireland, serving as master of ceremonies, addressed those assembled and announced that Mrs. W.J. Upson (1879–1955) had donated a flag for the post. F. Edward Hanscom was selected as assistant chief observer and Constance Philbrook as secretary. According to Daisy LeClair's diary, the post permanently closed in October 1943.

Fall meant election time in Maine (whose citizens voted in September and would for many more years). The liquor question was decided by a two-to-one margin in favor of keeping Bethel "dry" once more (perhaps the margin suggested another wartime sacrifice), and the Republican candidate for governor, Sumner Sewell, who had become well known for his wartime leadership, won the town by a margin of nearly three to one (294–102).

In December 1942, pleas for Russian relief that appeared in the *Citizen* received a positive response in Bethel. Much of this support came from schools; students apparently did not share the deep misgivings of their elders in assisting the brutal dictator of a Communist nation in its struggle against Hitler's invading armies. A response to the town's generosity was also received by the *Citizen* from a Royal Air Force serviceman in Iceland thanking Bethel people for a pair of knitted socks, which was much appreciated.

With the coming of the new year, thoughts turned to planting, and Pearl Ashby Tibbetts urged the creation of Victory Gardens. She headed the effort in Bethel to encourage the growing of a variety of vegetables on land near the Androscoggin off Bridge Street. Mrs. Tibbetts emphasized the desirability of obtaining good seed and of early planting. Her leadership resulted in attracting a number of gardeners anxious to do their bit for the town's war effort.

In the spring of 1943, it was directed by the federal government that slaughterhouses were to have permits in order to operate. This registration was resented in some Bethel quarters as another example of governmental meddling. Less controversial was the *Citizen*'s warnings that if bombs or mines were discovered, they were to be reported to authorities. The *Citizen* also attempted at this time to stifle the rumor that bobby pins were to be unavailable for the rest of the war. It added that wartime was one of the worst times for rumors and urged readers to be certain of the facts before passing on information.

To expedite the distribution of reliable information, a neighborhood plan was adopted, and Alberta Croteau was selected to head the effort. Assisting her in this program were women from many parts of the village or nearby, including Jane Van Den Kerckhoven, Ruth Chapman, Helen Connolly, Grace Chamberlain, Lilas Coolidge, Verna Dyke, Winona Davis, Lillian Smith, Celia Gorman, Elsie Davis and Marvel Hanscom. At the same time that the neighborhood plan was established, a Red Cross drive with a goal of $1,300 was being organized. Since Bethel had 1,300 voters, declared the *Citizen*, it would seem realistic to expect at least one dollar from each voter toward the cause.

If fundraisers appeared optimistic about money, other commodities were not so plentiful. Stovepipe was in very short supply in Bethel, and everyone who could was encouraged to use bicycles (Victory Bikes) as much as possible to save gasoline. Restrictions were tightening on coffee, fuel oil, sugar, meat and butter. By May 1943, however, rubber boots and tires for farm equipment were ration-free.

Amid all this activity, several Bethel women led by Grace Coburn (1900–1967) organized an auxiliary to the state guard, which later elected Stephanie Thurston (1914–1985) as captain of the group. Various other organizations helped outfit soldiers and sailors with uniforms, rifles and blankets. Among these (and their contributions) were the Rebekahs ($806.25), Eastern Star ($1,263), Women's Society for Christian Service ($93.75), American Legion Auxiliary ($525), Ladies Club and Junior Guild of the Congregational Church ($6,993.65) for a total of nearly $10,000.

By May 1943, the *Citizen* was reporting that the Civil Defense effort in Bethel was lacking support. Few had blackout curtains, and not everyone was doing his or her part in preserving precious commodities useful to the war effort. One bright spot seemed to be the raising of $5,000 by Bethel schools through the sale of bonds and stamps.

Schools were seen as part of the domestic war effort in Bethel, as was the case in many municipalities throughout the nation. Superintendent Carrie Wight proclaimed the school's role in the 1942 town report, noting that the "teachers have entered into the defense program of the community with a sense of patriotism." She reported that most of the teaching staff had taken "first aid and nurse's courses" and regretted "the loss of pupil's time from the classroom" to support the war effort. It was necessary, however, since "our first duty is to win the war," and she added, "considered in this light a few days' loss of school is nothing if the time sacrificed by the pupils will aid their safety for the future." Miss Wight viewed schools as "instruments for our defense in the future" to which "our loyalty…must not waver." On this occasion, she closed her remarks with the comment that school transportation might not for the foreseeable future be as convenient as parents would like, but changes were mandated by the federal government. She requested that both parents and pupils affected by these conditions "accept them as part of their contribution to the war program."

Two years later, in 1944, Superintendent Wight was able to report that the war had definitely affected the town's schools, with a critical shortage of teachers among the most pressing results. Nonetheless, she concluded her remarks that year with the following observation:

> *The teachers and pupils of Bethel have responded splendidly to the demands made upon the schools along different lines for winning the war. War bonds and stamps to the amount of over $10,000 have been purchased during the past year. The schools have had several paper collections bringing the total collected to 15 tons.*

Whether things were quite so rosy as Miss Wight suggested is not clear from the evidence. Nevertheless, one change that had a positive and lasting effect was the introduction of the school lunch program in the village schools during the 1942–43 academic year.

In addition to education, another daily vital service also experienced the effect of the war. By the summer of 1943, there were serious questions of whether Rural Free Delivery mail would have to be severely curtailed due to the rationing of gasoline. Albert Silver, carrier on RFD #2, found it impossible to deliver mail at times, and Earl Davis (1901–1977), mailman on RFD #1, was reported by the *Citizen* as "worried" about making his deliveries in the future.

During this period, there was a particularly strong emphasis on stretching scarce resources. A system of loans for pressure cookers was established. There was also a Victory Pulpwood campaign since wood was used in smokeless powder, in rayon for parachutes, plastic for plane parts, shell and bomb cases and shipping containers of ammunition, food, supplies, blood and plasma. The Extension Service provided instructions in using less fat and other strategic foods in cooking. There was also a shortage of surgical dressings, and several Bethel women, including Daisy LeClair, gathered at various Main Street locations during afternoons to roll bandages for use in the war.

By the fall of 1943, a can salvage campaign was begun with Henry Flint (1901–1951) as chairman, assisted by Elwood Ireland of Gould Academy and Doris Lord of the Bethel Grammar School. Detailed instructions were distributed as to how tin cans were to be flattened for use in the nation's defense program.

On another front, an army caravan appeared in Bethel about this time to emphasize the importance of wood in fighting fascism. Also bolstering Bethel's defense effort was the fact that the local state guard, now numbering some sixty members, had placed an order for a machine gun.

At the end of October 1943, the town was shocked with the news that Second Selectman John Howe and his cousin William Hastings of East Bethel, as well as the brother of D. Grover Brooks, had drowned in Umbagog

Lake. Among the mourners at the Howe-Hastings funeral at East Bethel Church was their first cousin, Canadian Cabinet Minister C.D. Howe from Ottawa, who had interrupted his leadership of Canada's war production program to come to Bethel for this sad occasion.

By 1944, it was reported that German prisoners of war were working in the woods near Milan, New Hampshire, for the Brown Paper Company of Berlin. Wood had, in fact, become such a strategic material that the Bethel railroad station was viewed as a vital shipping point. In addition, plans were made (but never executed) to greatly expand the rail facilities in the community so that even more wood might be transported from Bethel for wartime use. D-Day came in 1944, and with it the loss in France of Lawrence Perry of West Bethel. There was also in the same year a campaign in Bethel to collect milkweed pods for use in life jackets. In this case, twenty cents was being offered for each bag of eight hundred pods.

In the elections during the fall of 1944, Bethel selected Republican Horace Hildreth for governor by a vote of 309 to 60 for his Democratic opponent. The liquor question found the town voting once more for prohibition (this

Bethel Rebekahs gathered at the Odd Fellows Hall, Main Street, 1940s.

time by a 3–1 margin), and Bethel voters preferred Governor Thomas E. Dewey over President Roosevelt, 489 to 253.

By the beginning of 1945, attention began to turn toward the postwar period. Hopes were high that the war would soon be over and life might return to "normal." It was not to happen too soon, however, since Japan did not surrender until September 1945. Before that time, many of the wartime restrictions had disappeared. The *Citizen* carried the entire text of the proposed United Nations Charter, which was seen as the best hope for avoiding another catastrophic war. By April 1945, the local Lion's Club was collecting funds for European relief. The next month, James D. Alger was released, and by the fall the *Citizen* overseas edition had been suspended.

With the war ended, Bethel people, along with the rest of the world, rejoiced that at last the difficult years of conflict were over. Bethel had lost 15 sons, and several others had been wounded of the 270 Bethel men and women who served in the four branches of the service. All who returned home seemed anxious to get on with their lives, which had been so decisively disrupted by the war. The conflict had brought sacrifice and scarcity to Bethel, as it had to the nation. It had meant bond and scrap metal drives to support the United States defense effort. Inconvenience had come to many and profound grief to some, especially those with loved ones placed in harm's way. Some had received more restricted materials than others; "the black market" had worked in Bethel as it did in the nation, but on a greatly reduced scale. There had been some local inefficiency and disorganization in directing Bethel's response to the war, but nothing like that which had prevailed on the national level.

Bethel had few (if any) khaki-whackies (sloppily dressed teenage girls wearing bright red lipstick who flocked to men in uniform). Despite the best efforts of the Office of Price Administration, prices did rise sharply in the town (nationally about 47 percent between 1939 and 1945). Many Bethel people did listen to the radio (comedy shows such as Edgar Bergen and Charlie McCarthy, Jack Benny, Bob Hope and Fibber McGee and Molly were particularly favored), play board and card games and read paperbacks (extremely popular during the war years) like their counterparts throughout the nation. There were, however, few sandbags in attics or stirrup pumps under roofs in Bethel. Hoarding was a common form of recreation in this town, as it was nationally, despite the unpatriotic associations that its practice raised. Cigarettes were hard to obtain in Bethel as they were in much of the country. Bacon and cheese became almost a memory in Bethel. Attempts were made in this community, as was the case throughout the United States,

Main Street, Bethel Hill, 1950s.

to portray the American housewife as a soldier (like the men in combat overseas) preserving her kitchen's vital war resources.

A permanent legacy of the war that separated Bethel from some other communities was the development of a municipal airport, which became a reality in November 1945. This can be seen as one of the positive outcomes of a generally trying and turbulent era. The airport came out of a meeting in early 1945 at the *Citizen* office under the auspices of the Bethel Chamber of Commerce, where local enthusiasts drew up plans to build an airfield about a half-mile from Bethel Hill on what was then known as Northwest Bethel Road (now North Road). The group included Elmer Bennett, Warren Blake, Carl Brown and his son Edwin and Leslie Davis and his son Richard. By selling stock at $10 per share, the newly formed Bethel Airport Corporation raised a total of $4,210, which made it possible to construct a two-thousand-foot gravel runway. Land for the airport was donated by two businessmen, Fred Edwards and Henry Boyker. It was initially named for Edwards, and two hangars were constructed and operations commenced. For a time, interest was high and volunteers numerous. Many stumps were removed and brush cut.

By the 1950s, interest had waned and the airport needed funds for maintenance and property taxes. Later, Leslie Davis bought most of the shares and twenty-five acres and donated it for a runway. In addition, a twenty-year option was provided in case the Town of Bethel wished to expand the facility and establish a municipal airport. In 1959, a portion of the original acreage was sold and the proceeds used to dissolve the corporation, with the L.E. Davis Lumber Company retaining the residual land.

Activity at the airport declined until about 1963, when Errol, New Hampshire contractor Merritt Bean and Lieutenant Colonel Sidney Dyke proposed to Bethel's business interests that the airport needed upgrading. A number of improvements in grading and widening occurred, as well as the construction of an administrative building. In 1964, due to the work of Colonel Dyke and others, the airport was licensed by the state's Aeronautics Commission. Also at this time, Colonel Dyke offered flight instruction, and an underground fuel tank was installed as well as a fuel pump. During 1964 and 1965, the Town of Bethel re-graded the runway. Sadly, the following year, Colonel Dyke was killed in a plane crash. Richard Davis took over as airport manager until 1968, when Robert Lowe assumed the post.

In 1975, the Bethel town manager's responsibilities were expanded to include airport oversight. The fuel facilities were subsequently sold to Harold Clukey for private use. An Airport Advisory Committee was established by the board of selectmen to determine the future status of the airport, with Dexter Landers, a local businessman and pilot, as chair and Edwin Brown and John Head as members. The recommendation was to improve the facility, and a consultant was retained to provide some professional planning. In 1983, the Master Plan was narrowly approved at the annual town meeting. To raise the local match, an industrial park was created. In 1987, Richard Davis cleared the timber and the National Guard removed stumps and did initial grading for a new runway. Pike Industries paved the runway the following year at a cost of $2.4 million. The old airstrip became an aircraft parking apron and the site of an industrial park. In 1992, the Town of Bethel purchased the former GAMM building in the industrial park. American Skiing Company, led by Leslie B. Otten, moved to the GAMM building in 1997 and became a major influence in the airport's development, installing a lighting system that was eventually transferred to the town in 2003. Since that time, hangars have been built, the facilities upgraded and the runway expanded to 3,820 feet. In 1998, the name was changed to Bethel Regional Airport, Colonel Dyke Field.

Bennett's Garage and Head's Store at "Gander Corner," West Bethel, 1930s.

Prior to the development of an airport at the North Road site, West Bethel had been the location of the first Bethel airfield. Dean Cunningham, formerly with a California flying circus, offered lessons here. Also associated with this field were Elmer Bennett, Ray Crockett, Carmeno Onofrio and Harold Lurvey. These men and others struggled with finding a suitable field, using meadows on Vernon Street and on Intervale Road until 1930, when Clarence Bennett offered a site in back of his garage in West Bethel village. By 1931, the first hangar had been constructed. The landing field was marked "WB" in white sand, and "Bethel" was painted on the roof of a garage in that village.

The postwar era brought to Bethel, as it did the nation, a strong contempt for communism. Cold war mindsets by those at the highest levels of government led to war in Korea and Vietnam. These incursions had less impact upon Bethel than was the case with World War II, but sons were lost in each instance.

In the summer of 1949, Phyllis Smith suffered a serious accident when a homemade tractor she was driving slipped backward, causing her to fall off the seat. The tractor ran over her and caused serious injuries. To help her family out with medical expenses, Norma Jodrey and Beatrice Brown organized a community event that came to be known as the Bethel Bazaar. The first such event was held that summer on a then vacant lot at the corner of Main and Mechanic Streets. Since that time, the Bethel Bazaar has become a Bethel institution. In 1960, the name was changed to Molly Ockett Day, which is always held on the third Saturday in July. With a parade, booths on the Bethel Common, races and competitions, music and fireworks in the evening, the event is one of the outstanding community activities of each year in Bethel.

Emerging from the war, the town began to evolve further. The 1890s Brick Grammar School, near the academy, became increasingly inadequate, and a new school opened on the former Crescent grounds, known today as Crescent Park School. This school was significantly enlarged in 1994. The outlying schools in the east, west, south and north neighborhoods were all closed by the late 1960s.

The landscape of secondary education underwent seismic changes in the mid- to late 1960s when the trustees of Gould Academy announced that the school would no longer be the high school for Bethel-area residents. The Bingham Trust for Charity attempted to alleviate this disruption of a long tradition by offering a grant of $400,000 toward the construction of a new public high school, which was named Telstar Regional (after a satellite that transferred communications to a facility in Andover, Maine, a town in the newly created school district) after a spirited naming contest. Previously, in 1965, Bethel voters had joined the neighboring towns of Andover, Greenwood, Newry and Woodstock to create School Administrative District 44.

Change also came in the town's government. In 1953, the Bethel voters approved an article to increase the board of selectmen from three to five members and adopt the town manager form of government, to take effect in March 1954. The following year, the Village Corporation was dissolved. Oswald T. Rozelle was the first town manager, serving until 1957. His successors and their terms of office include Harold Bean (1957–62), Michael Houlihan (1962–67), Elwyn Dickey (1967–75), Harold Bean (acting, 1975), Norman Ness (1975–81), Merton Brown (acting, 1981–82), William Judson (1982–84), Dewey Thayer (acting, 1984–95), Rodney Lynch (1985–90), Madeleine Henley (1990–97), Phillip Tarr (1997–99), Scott Cole (1999–2009) and James Doar (2009–).

Town meetings have changed considerably since they were all-day affairs at Odeon Hall with a meal served at noon by Bethel Grange #56 at its hall on Spring Street. Lively discussions were standard fare in those days, and town officers were elected from the floor until the Australian ballot was adopted in 1937. In recent years, town meetings have been held at Telstar

Telstar Regional High School, located on the Walker's Mills Road south of Bethel Hill, opened in 1968.

Regional High School auditorium and, since the enlargement of Crescent Park School in the mid-1990s, at the gymnasium.

In politics, the town has been traditionally Republican since the founding of that party in the 1850s, but the margin of registered Republicans over Democrats has steadily declined. Independent voters have now become the largest voting group, with numbers exceeding each party's enrollment. Moreover, Bethel voters have sometimes exercised a spirit of independence, splitting tickets (particularly in recent years) and voting for Republicans Margaret Chase Smith and William S. Cohen as well as Democrats Edmund Muskie and George Mitchell.

Citizens of Bethel were pleased with President Lyndon B. Johnson's appointment in 1964 of Bethel native and Gould Academy 1937 valedictorian Margaret Joy Tibbetts as United States ambassador to Norway. Ms. Tibbetts was one of the first female career diplomats elevated to ambassadorial rank.

In 1947, four professors—Kurt Lewin, PhD, chairman of the faculty and director of the Research Center for Group Dynamics at the Massachusetts Institute of Technology; Ronald Lipitt, PhD, assistant

The National Training Laboratories (NTL) began at Gould Academy in 1947 and later purchased Dr. Gehring's former home for its headquarters.

professor of psychology at the Research Center for Group Dynamics at the Massachusetts Institute of Technology; Leland Bradford, PhD, director of adult education at Teachers College, Columbia University; and Kenneth D. Benn, PhD, associate professor of education at Teachers College, Columbia University—sought and obtained a grant from the Office of Naval Research to test some ideas regarding human interaction. With the support of the National Education Association, they looked for a place in New England, reasonably close to MIT, where travel costs for researchers would be minimal and that would be sufficiently isolated in order that a "cultural island" effect might be developed to assist in the training. Gould Academy in Maine was suggested and selected because of its high-quality facilities. Since that time, the National Training Laboratory (NTL) has held seminars at Gould and later at its own facilities, the former Dr. Gehring property, where the T-group process, sensitivity training and encounter groups were among the experiences offered to a worldwide clientele. As a result of NTL's presence in the town, Bethel became more cosmopolitan and gained the reputation as perhaps the best-known small town in the world for those involved in the social and behavioral sciences.

Another development with significant implications for Bethel's future was the opening in 1959 of the Sunday River Ski Area on Barker Mountain in Newry. Although the facility was located in a neighboring town, it was several Bethel businessmen and ski enthusiasts who organized the corporation, sold stock and oversaw its growth in the early years. Today, Sunday River has expanded dramatically to become one of the largest and best-known ski areas in the East. Skiing had come to Bethel by the 1920s, and for a time there was a modest ski slope on Robertson Hill that was used by Gould Academy students on land owned by John Anderson. It is not known when this site lost its attraction, but in the late 1940s a ski slope with a rope tow was developed on Vernon Street. This facility was closed when the move came to Barker Mountain. In fact, the rope that was used to bring skiers up the slope overlooking Vernon Street was transferred and used for a time at Sunday River. Another ski area in an adjoining town was also initially developed by businessmen residing in Bethel. That enterprise, Mount Abram in Greenwood, was the creation of the Cross brothers, Stuart, Donald and Norton. In the 1950s and 1960s, there was also a ski jump near Swan's corner maintained by Gould Academy as well as one in "Devil's Kitchen" during the 1930s. In recent years, the popularity of Nordic skiing in Bethel has also grown significantly.

Television is believed to have arrived in Bethel in 1949 when Ray Crockett installed a console in his garage window on lower Church Street. At that time, there were no stations in Maine and his set was tuned to one in Boston that only came in when the weather was favorable.

Bethel has always had a wide variety of organizations that have alternately flourished and languished through the years. In addition, there have been others, such as the Masonic Order, two Granges and a few others, that have existed in town for a century or more. A number of organizations, such as the Odd Fellows and Rebekahs, lasted nearly a century until changing times made them less popular with many citizens. For a brief time beginning in 1921, Bethel had a Knights of Pythias Lodge as well as the female counterpart, the Pythian Sisters. Both groups held their meetings in the Odd Fellows Hall. The American Legion Post (initially named for George Mundt but renamed Mundt-Allen by 1949) was founded in 1920. For many years, the post was on Main Street, but in the 1970s, the building was sold and the headquarters was moved to Vernon Street. In 1922, Edwin Barker organized a Farm Bureau in Bethel. Church youth groups and 4-H clubs (from the 1920s with such club names as Early Risers, Merry Toilers and Bethel Builders) attracted numerous members. For some time, the Lion's

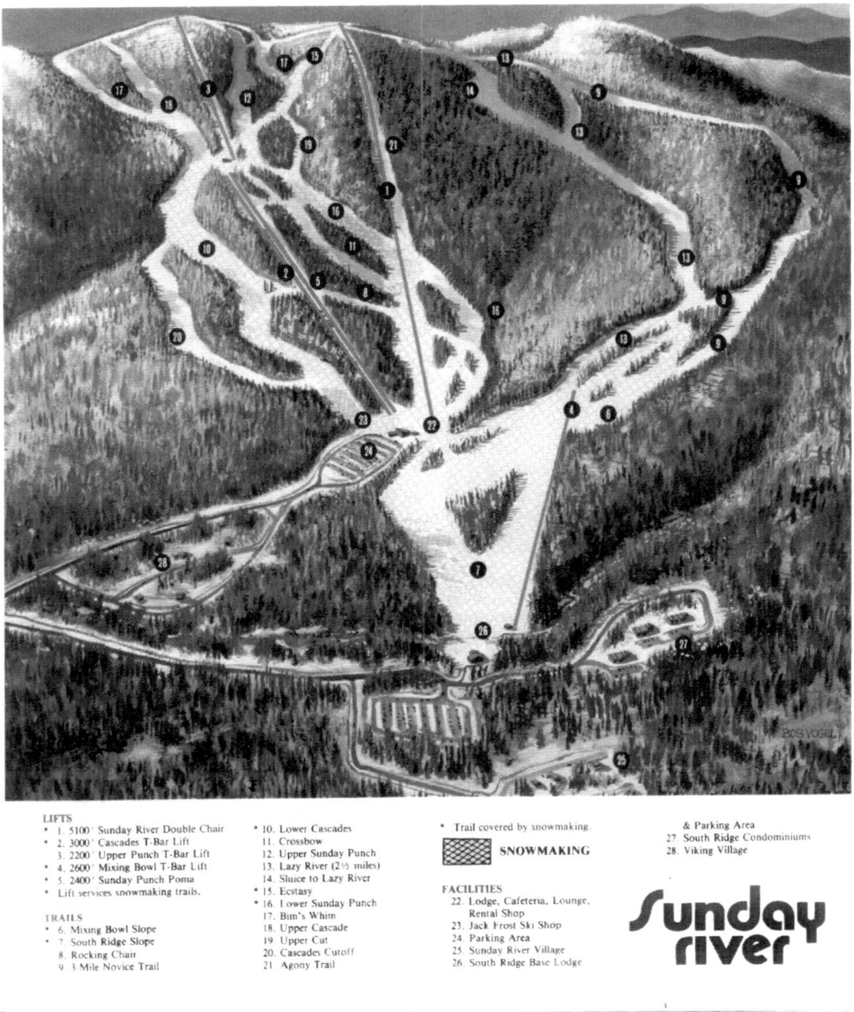

The Sunday River Ski Area in Newry, founded in 1959 by Bethel businessmen, grew rapidly under the leadership of Leslie B. Otten.

Club was also a popular organization in Bethel, but in recent years it has not been especially active. Relief organizations such as the Salvation Army were for years headed by Carl Brown. Other clubs and societies have had a short existence. Among these were the all-women History Club organized in 1897, the Mountain Ash Club, the Modern Woodmen of America and the Village Improvement Society led by Judge Addison Herrick in 1903.

One of the most ambitious self-improvement organizations that ever existed in Bethel was perhaps the Good Morals League, organized in 1904, which had the following pledge requirements:

1. *To abstain from the use of liquor;*
2. *To refrain from the use of profanity;*
3. *To refrain from gambling;*
4. *To refrain from loafing and rowdyism in public places;*
5. *To cultivate reverent speech and attitude towards sacred things;*
6. *If a minor, refrain from any use of tobacco in any form; if an adult, careful consideration of the morals before use;*
7. *To refrain from dishonesty, cheating, gossip, especially that injurious to character and from misrepresentations.*

Among those associated with this organization, which had ninety charter members, were publisher E.C. Bowler, Reverend Frank C. Potter of the Bethel Methodist Church and Frank E. Hanscom, principal of Gould's Academy.

Since the days of the famous Maine Law in 1851, Bethel has remained largely a "dry" town—at least officially. Alcohol was still available for "medicinal purposes" at the town liquor agency (operated for many years by Leander T. Barker on Main Street). At least a few skeptics believed that not all the liquor sales were for the intended purposes, and E.C. Bowler, owner of the *Bethel News*, thought that the customer list should be made public in order to gain greater compliance with the law. By the 1920s, guests at such hotels as the Bethel Inn got their desired alcoholic drinks with liquor purchased in New Hampshire by inn employees and surreptitiously supplied to a willing clientele. Since Bethel was relatively close to the Canadian border, there was a good chance that considerable rumrunning was occurring in this era as well. Some liquor agents were able to disrupt lines of supply, but much more undoubtedly made it through to waiting customers. Ninety-two gallons of illegal liquor were seized in 1925, for example, and the previous year, liquor agents discovered seventy-eight gallons of gin hidden near the Paradise Hill reservoir. Periodically there were reports of Bethel residents arrested for operating illegal stills. But these and the seizures must have been anomalies since, nationally and certainly locally, prohibition was not very effective. Under Carl Brown's ownership, the *Citizen* long stood on the side of prohibition, but the town finally voted in 1968 to allow liquor sales, which dramatically ended Bethel's experiment with alcoholic abstinence.

Anti-alcohol sentiment was not the only prejudice evident during the nineteenth and early twentieth centuries. Also present was intolerance involving ethnic groups and certain religions. In 1924, when the Ku Klux Klan was enjoying a national revival, Klan sentiment in Maine reached its height of popularity, largely due to a strong anti-immigrant and anti-Catholic bias. It was generally believed that the Republican Maine gubernatorial candidate Ralph Owen Brewster of Dexter was elected with Klan support, despite his assurances to the contrary. In July 1924, the KKK met at the Grange Hall on Spring Street with over 250 persons in attendance, according to an account in the *Citizen*. A few days later, on July 28, 1924, another Klan meeting was held in the Methodist church. No further mention of the Klan appears in the local newspaper, so it can be assumed that the revival of this organization in Bethel was a short-term development.

Another minor but interesting form of conflict in this period were the gas wars between competing filling stations. At any given time in the 1930s and 1940s, there might have been as many as six stations trying to attract business by lowering gas prices to unprofitable levels. Customers appeared to like this rivalry, but it was not always an easy time for proprietors.

No mines were ever operated in Bethel, but in surrounding towns, there existed extensive mining operations at one time or another. There were, however, two mining-related businesses based in Bethel in the 1950s. The Beryllium Development Corporation of Reading, Pennsylvania, which operated out of an office on Church Street, sold beryllium, used in defense and industrial production, from mines in Greenwood and Newry and shipped to market by rail from Bethel. Roger and Chester Wheeler of West Bethel operated a mica processing shop on Main Street in Bethel in the late 1950s on the site of today's Northeast Bank. The mica came from mining operations in Gilead and was used in appliances.

Two organizations that were founded in the 1960s and have played an important role in Bethel life since that time were the Bethel Senior Citizens, formed in 1962 by such individuals as Emily Saunders, Sarah Stevens and Virginia Walker, and the Bethel Historical Society, which came into being under the leadership of Eva M. Bean in 1966.

Writings about Bethel have been numerous through the years. Dr. N.T. True was one of the most prolific contributors in newspapers such as the *Portland Transcript*, and his nineteenth-century history of Bethel, compiled, edited and published in book form by Randall Bennett, appeared in 1994. The famous writer Harriet Beecher Stowe recorded in 1852 some observations of life in Bethel and the surrounding countryside. Lucy Larcom, one of

Eva M. Bean, author of *East Bethel Road* and, in 1966, the leading founder of the Bethel Historical Society.

the most famous nineteenth-century literary figures in New England, spent many summers in Bethel, where mountain vistas inspired her poetic writing. Henry T. Finck, music critic for the *New York Post*, authored several books on music, and in his *My Adventures in the Golden Age of Music* (1926) wrote glowingly of Bethel, giving the town credit for his being able to accomplish so much during the summer since he was "breathing the health-giving exhilarating air of the Maine mountains." Ruth Crosby's *I Was a Summer Boarder*, published in 1966, recorded her nostalgic memories of a Bethel boardinghouse and its guests, including Henry T. Finck. Her *From an Old Leather Trunk*, which appeared in 1974, also contains numerous references to her beloved Bethel. Erma Thurston Young's *Yesterday and Today* (1953) presents memories of the Bethel area at the beginning of the twentieth century. In his *The Gould Academy Story*, published in 1976, Francis Parkman produced a work of much interest for those intrigued with the history of that significant Bethel institution. Joan S. Kilborn's *Over the Horizon* (1950) contains some revealing insights into Bethel's "town characters." Mina Holway Caswell wrote a highly useful biography of William Rogers Chapman that was published in 1938. In 1904, Harriette F. Farwell produced a compilation of genealogical information in her *Shaw Records*, which was printed in Bethel and contains useful data on local families. In his *Experiment in Medicine*, which appeared in 1960, Joseph E. Garland provided a valuable history of the Pratt Diagnostic Clinic with details relating to Bethel, Gehring and Bingham.

Literary works with connections to Bethel include longtime resident Pearl Ashby Tibbetts's novel *Land Under Heaven*, which was written in Bethel but set in her native Aroostook County. Children's books have been written by Bethel people, including Phyllis Dock (*Little Hawk*, 1967) and Susan Clement Farrar (*Samantha on Stage*, 1979). There have been a number of books of fiction believed to be inspired by a Bethel setting, including Robert Herrick's *Master of the Inn* (1911) and William Andrews's *Stealing History* (2006).

In recent years, Bethel has been utilized as a setting for several films, including *The Myth of Fingerprints* and *The Twelve Dogs of Christmas*. In the early 1980s, Bethel Hill village served as the backdrop for a nationally televised Hallmark Greeting Card commercial.

Bethel at mid-century was a blend of the past and what became more common as the twentieth century wore on. The Gould Academy of yesteryear assumed a new role as an independent school without large numbers of students from the town of Bethel and other outlying areas (and their tuition). Telstar Regional High School opened in 1968 and graduated its first class the following year. This change was due to a variety of factors, including the reluctance on the part of Gould Academy trustees to provide vocational opportunities for some students, and was arguably the most significant consequence of these years. No longer would the townspeople focus on the academy as they had for over 130 years. A new relationship would evolve with that institution while a challenging and exciting world of public education was created and continues to unfold at Telstar Regional High School.

Chapter Five

BETHEL TRANSFORMED

In 1974, the Bethel Savings Bank left its space in the Cole Block that it had occupied since the 1890s to move to its new brick building next door. Symbolically, it was one of many changes that marked a new era in Bethel history, where a simpler way of life gave way to a new corporate style of commerce and economic activity, a state of affairs that would begin to become routine in the late twentieth and the beginning of the twenty-first centuries.

Also that same year, the Dr. Moses Mason House was dedicated and opened as a museum by the Bethel Historical Society, which earlier had received the generous support of the William Bingham II Trust for Charity to fund its acquisition and restoration. The gift of this building by the trust made it possible to display and store artifacts, hold events, do research and begin the work of bringing historical publications and programming to Bethel and the area. Historian Stanley R. Howe, a Bethel native and Gould graduate, was selected as site administrator that year. Since that time, the society has gained over 1,400 members, built an endowment, published several major books, added another building, increased its staff and expanded its reputation as one of the leading historical agencies in the state. Its numerous accomplishments have been recognized by both state and national organizations.

In addition, the Bethel Rotary Club was founded in 1974. Since that time, it has been a major presence in the town, serving to advance many good causes. In 2005, it presented to the town a classic street clock located near the local Key Bank.

With the greater interest in the environment in the 1970s, the town applied in 1971 for federal funding to build a wastewater treatment plant, thereby

Donated in 2005 by the Rotary Club of Bethel in honor of the Rotary's founding in 1905, this clock keeps Bethel's official time.

bringing to an end the longtime practice instituted at the beginning of the century of dumping raw sewerage into the Androscoggin. Sincc that timc, with several upgrades, the plant, located just below Bethel Hill, has been instrumental in bringing the river back as a major recreational resource for the area. Also assisting in the improvement of the river's water quality is the alleviation of industrial waste dumping from the west in Berlin and Gorham, New Hampshire, and east in Rumford and beyond from papermaking mills. Such activities as canoeing and fishing are becoming increasingly popular on the Androscoggin once again.

Another development in the 1970s was the growth of interest in adult and community education sponsored by the local school district. Emphasizing that education is a lifelong process, Bethel residents, along with their counterparts in the other district towns, have acquired high school diplomas and college credit, or learned new skills and enriched their lives with more diverse perspectives and learning experiences.

During the national bicentennial observance in 1976, a special events committee, chaired by Robert Keniston, was established. The committee

Since the 1970s, Bethel's Wastewater Treatment Plant has been reducing the town's impact on the Androscoggin River's water quality.

planned a number of activities and was instrumental in getting an article introduced into the town meeting warrant to establish a Recreation Board to coordinate Bethel's recreational programs. As a result, baseball, swimming, cross-country skiing and other activities continue to involve a large number of Bethel youth. Also established in 1976 was a historic marker system by the Bethel Historical Society. The first site so named was Bartlett Cemetery, believed to be the town's earliest cemetery, whose origins may extend back to 1780.

Six years later, Bethel commemorated the bicentenary of "New England's last Indian raid" with much fanfare and included many of those who were present at the last observance of this milestone in 1931. A square dance on Friday evening served to kick off the event, followed by a settlers' breakfast on Saturday morning. A cannon salute a bit later signaled the start of festivities. During the morning, exhibits opened and traditional crafts demonstrations commenced at Gould Academy, the Dr. Moses Mason House, General Alger's barn and on the grounds in back of the O'Neil Robinson House. A horse show also began off Bridge Street near the Androscoggin. A special blacksmith shop built for the event housed Albert Skillings's blacksmith demonstration, assisted by his grandson, Tim Korhonen. Also noteworthy was the demonstration by Alden Kennett and his son Edward of carpentry techniques of another era, including rail fence making, shake splitting and mortise and tenon construction. An art show organized by Helen Morton featuring a number of local artists opened on the Hastings Homestead lawn.

A spectacular heritage parade got underway in the late morning, preceded by militia units from all over New England as well as participants from Quebec and New York State. Following them was a color guard from the Mundt-Allen and Jackson Silver American Legion Posts. Retired U.S. Army lieutenant general James D. Alger, who served as honorary chairman, was accompanied by State Representative Karen Brown of Bethel and Indian Raid '81 coordinator Stanley R. Howe at the head of the parade. Over twenty elaborately crafted floats were evaluated by judges Albert Brown, Stuart Martin and Alice Johnson. Music was provided by bands from Bridgton and Buckfield.

After the parade, there were canoe races at Songo Pond. Militia demonstrations on the Bethel Common were enjoyed during the afternoon. They included an Indian raid and a mock battle employing eighteenth-century techniques, which was a real crowd pleaser. Bean suppers in the evening were held in three locations and were followed by a jam session on the Bethel Common with a heritage film and slide lecture on the 1725 battle of Lovewell Pond by Crosby Millman of Gardiner.

Sunday morning began with an old-fashioned church service at the Congregational church. This was followed by a cannon volley and an eighteenth-century obstacle race on the Bethel Common. At noon, there was a children's parade and then the pageant, which took the form of a dramatic reading by Edward H. Hastings with action by militia groups. The finale of the event was a firing squad "execution" of a certain "green recruit" for insubordination, staged by the militia and Indian Raid '81 coordinator Howe.

One of the major concerns of the 1970s in Bethel was the absence of a general medical practitioner. Prior to this time, Bethel had always been able to attract a doctor, and for most of its previous history it was home to several. But as physicians such as Widd B. Twaddle and Raymond R. Tibbetts died or retired, retaining a resident physician was becoming increasingly problematic. After several years of effort with a federal grant, the situation was finally eased in 1978 with the opening of the Bethel Area Health Center, which was staffed by a resident physician as well as other medical personnel. The health center was initially located on Main Street at the former Samuel Philbrook house, but later moved to a 1960s building originally opened as an A&P Store. It stands on the lot that once included the homesite of one of Bethel's best-known and earliest architects, Thomas Holt.

Accompanying the dilemma regarding doctors in Bethel was the situation regarding an ambulance. Since the 1920s, the town had relied

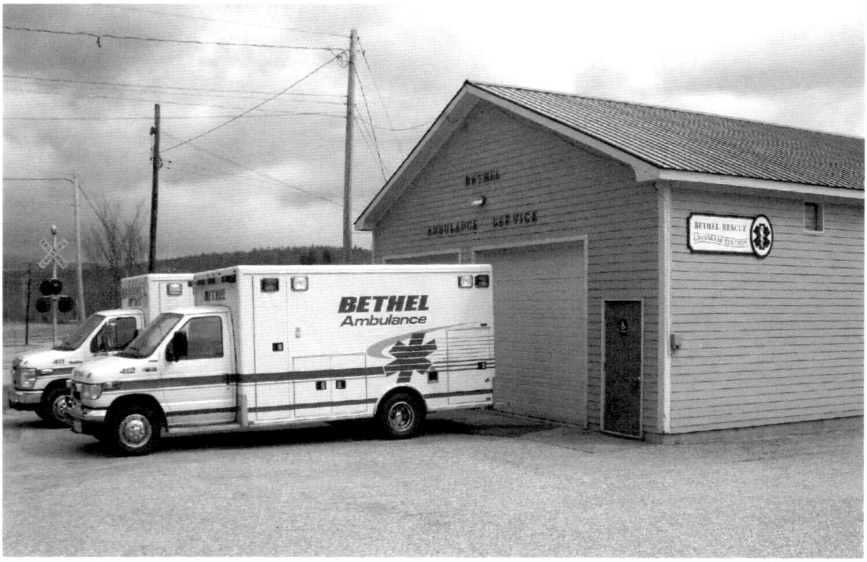

Dedicated in 2005 in honor of the Greenleaf family, the Bethel Emergency Ambulance and Rescue Service facility is an important town department.

on Dr. S.S. Greenleaf, the local veterinarian and funeral director, whose hearse also served as the town's ambulance. After Dr. Greenleaf's death in 1962, his son continued to operate the funeral home, but state and federal regulations regarding ambulances brought an end to the hearse/ambulance arrangement. The dilemma was solved in 1975 by the formation of the Bethel Emergency Ambulance and Rescue Service (BEARS), a volunteer group that continues to operate this vital function out of a new facility at the foot of Main Street named in 2005 for the Greenleaf family.

Promotion of the town's numerous natural attractions and man-made amenities began about the beginning of the twentieth century largely by the Bethel Board of Trade. A special brochure with a cover photo of the Androscoggin River, intervales and mountains, as viewed through what appears to be a colonial revival entrance, directed readers to Edward King, secretary of the Bethel Board of Trade, for "any further information" on "Hotel and Boarding House rates or openings for new industries." Later, this organization became the Bethel Chamber of Commerce, which has evolved into more of a regional organization that is now called the Bethel Area Chamber of Commerce. This group currently has an office in the Bethel Station project. Led by its longtime executive director, Robin Zinchuk, the chamber has been zealous in marketing and promoting the

The world's tallest snowwoman was created in Bethel in 2007 and named in honor of Maine's U.S senator, Olympia Snowe. *Courtesy of the Bethel Area Chamber of Commerce and the* Bethel Citizen.

town and the region. Among its most ambitious and attention-getting projects in recent years was the building in 1999 of the world's tallest snowman (over 113 feet high), named for then Maine governor Angus King and introduced to the world as "Angus, King of the Mountain." The chamber later did something even more impressive by breaking its own *Guiness Book* record, with a giant snowwoman, named by popular demand for Maine's own U.S. senator, Olympia J. Snowe, that rose to over 122 feet in height. Both Governor King and Senator Snowe appeared in Bethel to visit these remarkable attractions that netted Bethel many thousands of dollars' worth of outstanding publicity.

The 1960s commenced a period of moving toward some kind of collective regulation of land use in the town, which would have seemed revolutionary in an earlier era when the fate of one's property was decided solely by its owner. A short-lived zoning ordinance enacted in the late 1950s, however, was repealed in 1968 after considerable controversy. Regulations for subdivisions and other local and state laws and municipal ordinances began to take effect in Bethel in the 1970s, and particularly after the town's acceptance of a comprehensive plan in 1979. A Planning Board was instituted, which reviewed proposals and decided future development projects in conformity with town, state and federal requirements. As time has passed, these regulations have become increasingly stricter due to environmental, aesthetic and safety concerns. One of the outgrowths of this increased interest in land use was the founding (by Kirk Siegel, Marcel Polak and others) of the Mahoosuc Land Trust in 1989. Based in Bethel, this entity has led the movement to acquire land or at least secure protective covenants to safeguard it from development and keep it accessible to the public.

Subsidized housing arrived in Bethel in 1976 with the construction of Sudbury Village. Since that time, there have been other similar projects added to the mix of housing options.

For generations, town dumps had often involved the Androscoggin River in an era when raw sewerage and nearly anything else that was to be disposed of finally ended up in the river. This situation began to change in the 1960s, when the municipal dump was moved from the mouth of Alder River to a site across from the town farm. In 1977, this dumping area became a sanitary landfill, which later evolved into, and remains today, a transfer station for the towns of Bethel, Newry and Hanover.

Due to the leadership of Gould Academy's Harry "Dutch" Dresser, Gould was one of the first independent schools in the nation to be connected to the Internet; this occurred during the fall of 1992. By the end of 1995, Bethel Data Corporation and Net Express offered dial-up access to any individual or entity. Dr. Dresser is also believed to be the first person to own a personal computer in Bethel, acquiring it in 1979.

As the end of the twentieth century came into view, Bethel's mills and wood products industries began to disappear. Once a vibrant element of the local economy, by the end of the first decade of the twenty-first century, there was but one sawmill left. The number of active farms also declined precipitously until today there are fewer than half a dozen that yield any commercial agricultural produce.

This children's band gathered on Main Street in the 1890s to promote a theatrical performance in Bethel. *Author's collection.*

While declines in Bethel have presumably been more noticeable in recent years than instances of growth, the number of businesses catering to tourists and other visitors appears to have increased. Restaurants, specialty shops for such items as furniture and pottery, cross-country skiing facilities, bed-and-breakfasts, realtors and commercial builders are more numerous than they were in 1950.

On the cultural front, Bethel has had a long tradition of interest in cultural activities, ranging from singing schools and later concerts in Ideal Hall in the nineteenth century to Mrs. Gehring's Columbian Club in the early twentieth century to the theatre performances of the Bethel Players in the 1950s. As an outcome of a community conference in the mid-1980s, the Mahoosuc Arts Council was formed in 1986 to provide a wide variety of community cultural performance activities for all ages.

The 1980s and 1990s proved to be a golden age for publishing books about the history of Bethel or the Bethel region. First to lead in this movement was the republication of William B. Lapham's *History of Bethel*, originally published in 1891 and brought out again in 1981 by New England History Press with new indices and an introductory essay by Stanley R. Howe containing a brief overview of Bethel since Lapham's time. Three years later, Randall Bennett's *Oxford County Maine: A Guide to Its Historic Architecture* was published by the Oxford County Historic Resource Survey, which was based at the Bethel Historical Society and funded by a federal grant administered by the Maine Historic Preservation Commission. That same year, Eva M. Bean's *East Bethel Road*, which first appeared in 1959, was reissued with over three hundred pages of updates. In 1991, *Bethel Maine: An Illustrated History* by Randall Bennett was published as the first comprehensive history of the town since Lapham's. In 1995, the Bethel Historical Society published Herbert P. Shirrefs's *The Richardson Lakes: Jewels in the Rangeley Chain*, which was edited by Randall H. Bennett. The society's quarterly, the *Bethel Courier* (the name was shortened in 1999 to the *Courier* in order to emphasize the more regional focus of the organization), continues to publish articles, book reviews and historical photographs on Bethel and the area.

Accompanying this "flowering" of publication was interest in historic preservation. Much of Bethel's built environment from the nineteenth and early twentieth centuries has survived largely intact. Led by the Bethel Historical Society in the 1970s, the Broad Street Historic District was created in 1977 and placed on the National Register of Historic Places. It included buildings in a wide variety of styles ranging from the elegant Federal to the eclectic Queen Anne. This district was later expanded to include

Gould Academy's McLaughlin Science Center was dedicated in 2002 and is currently the newest building on the campus.

structures on Church Street and those around Kimball Park, a nineteenth-century example of planned development. Generally, historic preservation has been valued in Bethel, as the town's architectural heritage remains a major attraction for visitors. Regrettably, there have been significant losses, including the removal of the town's 1865 railroad depot in 1968 and the razing in 2007 of the former home of Dr. John Grover, a signer of the Maine constitution. Another visual loss was the stately elms that once graced the village and the common that were cut down in the 1960s due to an onslaught of Dutch elm disease.

Planning for Bethel's bicentenary of incorporation began in 1993, with regular monthly meetings to plan a whole series of events designed to make the bicentennial year a thoroughly memorable one. Funds were raised, including a modest appropriation from the Town of Bethel, through a number of means, among them a Patriot's Day program, a "Belles and Brides" fashion show, raffles, benefit suppers and the sale of souvenirs (calendars, bronze medals, sweatshirts, pins, magnets and barn posters). A contest to develop a town logo attracted much attention, with a design by

Log drive on the Androscoggin River at Bethel, circa 1900. *Author's collection.*

In the 1920s and 1930s, the toboggan slide at the Bethel Inn was one of the town's most exciting winter attractions.

Don Katlin being selected and adopted to appear on all souvenir items as well as the town stationery. Activities throughout the year included exhibits, an art show, a veterans' "show and tell," lectures, a canoe flotilla, special postal cancellation day, an NTL lawn party, a Civil War encampment weekend, a pageant, a parade, fireworks, children's games, concerts and a house and garden tour. Woodland Cemetery was adopted as an official project of the Bicentennial Committee, which revitalized the historic graveyard's governing organization and began the process of reclaiming a neglected but highly significant burial ground. One of the other substantial accomplishments of the bicentennial year was securing a "home" for the historic fire bell that once hung in the tower of the old fire station dating from 1865. When that building was demolished in 1965, the bell was rescued but did not gain a proper placement until the bicentennial year, when the Bicentennial Committee, working closely with the fire department, designed a bell tower based on a drawing of the former station belfry by Danna Nickerson. It was placed on the north end of the Bethel Common and officially rededicated on June 10, 1997, exactly one year after the town's 200th anniversary was observed.

As the millennium passed in 2001, Bethel came increasingly under siege (in some observers' eyes) by the aggressive subdivision of forestland on the hills and mountains of the town. A real estate and building boom in the twenty-first century left a number of longtime residents with the feeling that the town was being transformed beyond recognition. Newcomers were arriving in Bethel regularly, and "natives" in certain quarters were feeling dismayed that they knew fewer and fewer people as they ventured to the post office or the grocery store. New energy and more diverse perspectives, however, were being added to the sense of place in Bethel by these new arrivals. In addition, a greater emphasis on fitness and well-being in the town brought the proposal and partial implementation of a trail system that is beginning to work its way in several directions from Bethel Hill village. This appears to be increasingly a direction that the town is taking, once more emphasizing the restorative qualities of a Bethel experience, harkening back to the days of Dr. Gehring, when so many visitors came to the town seeking a "cure" for their anxieties and stresses.

BIBLIOGRAPHY

PRIMARY

This history is largely based on research using a variety of newspapers, including the *Bethel Courier* (1858–61), the *Oxford Democrat* (1850s–1933), the *Oxford Advertiser* (1880s–1933), the *Bethel News* (1895–1908), the *Bethel Citizen* (1908–2008), the *Advertiser-Democrat* (1933–2007) and various news clippings from the *Portland Transcript*, the *Boston Post* and other regional newspapers.

Several oral histories collected by the Bethel Historical Society have been consulted as well.

Also used during the research for this book are diaries, letters, memoirs, atlases, census data, photographs, directories and other contemporary references in the custody of the Bethel Historical Society, the author or others.

Bethel News, Extra Illustrated Edition. January 6, 1904.

Bethel News. June 10, 1896. (Contains numerous articles relating to the centenary of Bethel's incorporation in 1796.)

The Bethel Oxford County Citizen Illustrated Edition Published in Observance of the Bicentennial of the First Settlement of Bethel. And to Commemorate the Dedication of the Moses Mason House Museum. Bethel, Maine, July 10, 1974.

Halfpenny, H.E., and John W. Caldwell. *Atlas of Oxford County, Maine.* Philadelphia: Caldwell and Halfpenny, 1880.

Herrick, Robert. *The Master of the Inn.* New York: Charles Scribner's Sons, 1911.

King, Thomas Starr. *The White Hills: Their Legends, Landscapes, and Poetry.* Boston: Chick and Andrews, 1859.

Lapham, William B. *My Recollections of the War of the Rebellion.* Augusta, ME: Burleigh & Flint, Printers, 1892.

Oxford County Citizen Illustrated Edition Published in Observance of the 150th Anniversary of the Last Indian Raid in Bethel, Maine, August 3, 1931.

Report of the Centennial Celebration at Bethel. Portland, ME: B. Thurston and Company, 1874.

Re-Union of the Students of Dr. Nathaniel T. True, at Gould's Academy, Bethel, Maine, Friday Afternoon and Evening, February 22, 1884. Gorham, NH: Mountaineer Print, 1884.

Re-Union Poems as Written and Delivered by A.S. Twitchell of Gorham, New Hampshire. Gorham, NH: V.V. Twitchell, 1883.

Segar, Nathaniel. *A Brief Narrative of the Captivity and Sufferings of Lt. Nathan'l Segar, Who Was Taken Prisoner by the Indians and Carried to Canada, During the Revolutionary War, Written by Himself.* Paris, ME: Oxford Bookstore, 1825.

The Town Register Greenwood, Bethel, Hanover, Woodstock, Gilead. Brunswick: Maine Map and Register Company, 1911.

True, Dr. Nathaniel Tuckerman. *The History of Bethel, Maine.* Bowie, MD: Heritage Books, 1994.

Willey, Reverend Benjamin G. *Incidents in White Mountain History.* Boston: Nathaniel Noyes, 1856.

SECONDARY

Significant secondary source information on Bethel's history is found in various issues of the Bethel Historical Society's quarterly, the *Courier*, from 1976 to the present.

Andrews, William. "Dr. John George Gehring and his Bethel Clinic: Pragmatic Therapy and Therapeutic Tourism." *Maine History* 43, no. 3 (January 2008): 188–216.

Bean, Eva M. *East Bethel Road.* Bethel, ME: Citizen Printers, 1959.

Bennett, Randall H. *Bethel, Maine: An Illustrated History.* Bethel, ME: Bethel Historical Society, Inc., 1991.

———. *Oxford County, Maine: A Guide to Its Historic Architecture.* Bethel, ME: Oxford County Historic Resource Survey, 1984.

The Bethel Oxford County Citizen Illustrated Edition Published in Observance of the Bicentennial of the First Settlement of Bethel. And to Commemorate the Dedication of the Moses Mason House Museum. July 10, 1974.

Bethel's Broad Street. Bethel, ME: Bethel Historical Society, 1977.

Calloway, Colin G. *The Western Abenaki of Vermont, 1600–1800: War, Migration, and the Survival of an Indian People.* Norman: University of Oklahoma Press, 1990.

Caswell, Mina Holway. *Ministry of Music: The Life of William Rogers Chapman.* Portland, ME: Southworth-Anthoenson Press, 1938.

Chapman, Leonard Bond. "Fragments of Local History." *Oxford County Citizen*, 1909–14.

Clark, Charles. *The Eastern Frontier: The Settlement of Northern New England, 1610–1763.* New York: Alfred A. Knopf, 1970.

Clark, Charles E., James S. Leamon and Karen Bowden, eds. *Maine and the Early Republic.* Hanover, NH: University Press of New England, 1988.

Crosby, Ruth. *I Was A Summer Boarder.* Boston: Christopher Publishing Company, 1966.

Day, Clarence A. *Farming in Maine, 1860–1940.* Orono: University of Maine Press, 1963.

———. *History of Maine Agriculture, 1604–1860.* Orono: University of Maine Press, 1954.

The Family Farm. Bethel, ME: Bethel Historical Society, 1975.

Haines, Agnes H., and Mildred O. Jackson, comp. *Bethel, Maine Cemeteries: A Listing of Gravestone Inscriptions Compiled by Agnes H. Haines and Mildred O. Jackson with an Introduction by Stanley Russell Howe.* Bethel, ME: Bethel Historical Society, 1989.

Howard, Alfred. *A History of Hanover, Maine, 1774–1980 with Associated Historical Events.* Manchester, ME: privately printed, 1983.

Howe, Stanley Russell. *Dr. Moses Mason and His House.* Bethel, ME: Bethel Historical Society, 1981.

———. *"A Fair Field and No Favor": A Concise History of the Maine State Grange.* Augusta: Maine State Grange, 1994.

Hubka, Thomas C. *Big House, Little House, Back House, Barn: The Connected Farm Buildings of New England.* Hanover, NH: University Press of New England, 1984.

Jones, Page Helm. *Evolution of a Valley: The Androscoggin River Story.* Canaan, NH: Phoenix Publishing Company, 1975.

Kilborn, Joan S. *Over the Horizon: Vignettes of a Voyager.* Portland, ME: A Dirigo Edition, 1950.

Kilbourne, Frederick. *Chronicles of the White Mountains.* New York: Houghton Mifflin Company, 1916.

Lapham, William B. *History of Bethel, Formerly Sudbury Canada, Oxford County, Maine, 1768–1890 with a Brief Sketch of Hanover and Family Statistics.* Augusta: Press of the Maine Farmer, 1891.

———. *History of the Town of Bethel, Maine: A Facsimile of the 1891 Edition with a New Historical Essay by Stanley Russell Howe.* Somersworth, NH: New England History Press, 1981.

Made in Bethel: A History of Mills and Manufacturing in Bethel, Maine 1774–1976. Bethel, ME: Bethel Historical Society, 1976.

Morrison, Kenneth M. *The Embattled Northeast: The Elusive Ideal of Alliance in Abenaki-European Relations.* Los Angeles: University of California Press, 1984.

Newell, Catherine S-C. *Molly Ockett.* Bethel, ME: Bethel Historical Society, 1981.

Parkman, Francis. *The Gould Academy Story.* Bethel, ME: Gould Academy, 1976.

Robinson, William F. *Mountain New England: Life Past and Present.* Boston: Little, Brown, 1988.

Shirrefs, Herbert P. *The Richardson Lakes: Jewels in the Rangeley Chain.* Bethel, ME: Bethel Historical Society, 1995.

Smith, David C. *A History of Lumbering in Maine, 1861–1960.* Orono: University of Maine Press, 1972.

Wight, Denman B. *The Androscoggin River Valley: Gateway to the White Mountains.* Rutland, VT: Charles E. Tuttle Company, 1967.

———. *The Wild River Wilderness: A Saga of Northern New England.* Littleton, NH: privately printed, 1971.

Wilkins, Martha F. *Sunday River Sketches: A New England Chronicle.* Rumford, ME: Androscoggin Publications, 1977.

Wood, Richard G. *A History of Lumbering in Maine, 1820–1861.* Orono: University of Maine Press, 1961.

Young, Erma Thurston. *Yesterday and Today.* Manchester, ME: A Dirigo Edition, 1953.

ABOUT THE AUTHOR

Stanley Russell Howe is a Bethel native with family ties to the town that extend back to the 1770s and the founding of the town. A graduate of Gould Academy and the University of Southern Maine, he also holds graduate degrees in history from the Universities of Connecticut (MA) and Maine (PhD). He became executive director of the Bethel Historical Society in 1974 and was selected in 1980 for the prestigious Seminar for Historical Administration, then based in Colonial Williamsburg. Very active professionally, he has lectured and written widely on New England and Canadian history topics and been a visiting lecturer at several universities. Currently chair of the Bethel Board of Selectmen, he also serves as a volunteer in a half dozen local and regional organizations and has received several awards for his long record of community service.